Personal Holiness

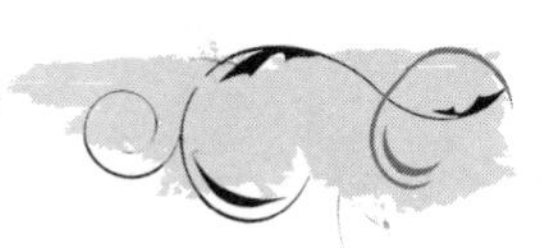

Personal Holiness

A Biblical Study for Developing a Holy Lifestyle

"A Woman's Guide" Series —Revised Edition

Rhonda Harrington Kelley

Birmingham, Alabama

New Hope Publishers
P. O. Box 12065
Birmingham, AL 35202–2065
www.newhopepublishers.com
New Hope® Publishers is a division of WMU®.

Library of Congress Cataloging-in-Publication Data

Kelley, Rhonda.
[Woman's guide to personal holiness]
Personal holiness : a biblical study for developing a holy lifestyle : a woman's guide / Rhonda H. Kelley.
p. cm.
Originally published: A woman's guide to personal holiness. c2000.
Includes bibliographical references.
ISBN 978-1-59669-257-2 (sc)
1. Christian women--Religious life. 2. Holiness--Biblical teaching. 3. Bible--Textbooks. I. Title.
BV4527.K443 2010
248.8'43--dc22

2010006951

ISBN-10:1-59669-257-X
ISBN-13: 978-1-59669-257-2

N104128 • 0610 • 2M1

~ TABLE OF CONTENTS ~

~ PREFACE ~

Only a few minutes of reading the paper or watching the news is needed to remind us of the sinfulness of human nature. God assures me that He is my only hope for godliness and that godliness should be a priority in my life. I have made a commitment to God, a commitment to myself, a commitment to my loved ones, and a commitment to you to be a godly woman. But I am reminded daily of my need to continually recommit myself to righteous living.

Holiness is a frequent theme of Scripture and a recurrent teaching for Christians. But holiness does not just happen. Holiness must be taught and sought! A study of God's Word will teach about His holiness and give instruction in daily holiness, but each follower of Christ must make a personal commitment to a life of holiness on a daily basis.

The Holy Spirit begins His work in the life of the believer when she is convicted of her sin and her need for salvation. He continues His work in the life of the believer convicting her of sinful behavior, guiding her in life decisions, empowering her in spiritual service, and providing for her personal needs. A study of Scripture and godly examples can promote righteousness. But a believer must depend on God alone and the power of His Spirit to develop and maintain a life of holiness.

While some Christians desire to be holy, others are less committed to the pursuit of holiness. Some Christian women even dread a life of holiness, thinking it means a life of rules and regulations or a daily routine of boredom. Nothing could be further from the truth. A believer's life need not be filled with negative discouragements, but positive encouragements. A woman of holiness learns to find great joy and satisfaction in her personal relationship with Jesus Christ. C. S. Lewis said, "How little people know who think that holiness is dull. When one meets the real thing . . . it is irresistible."

Join me in this biblical study of holiness. Experience the irresistible as you make a daily commitment to a lifestyle of personal holiness!

—Rhonda Harrington Kelley

~ INTRODUCTION ~

For hundreds of years, Christians have spoken of holiness but many have not lived holy lives! Now it is time to return to the Scripture for instruction in holiness. It is time to stop talking and begin living holy lives in an unholy world. We need righteousness for our sakes personally, and the world needs our godly witness.

This Bible study contains 12 lessons that examine the holiness of God and suggest guidelines for holy living. It is a topical study incorporating Old and New Testament passages about our Holy God and holy living. A variety of sources have been used in preparing this study to provide a comprehensive examination of this critical issue. In order to benefit from this study, several steps are essential.

1. **Commit to holiness.** First you must realize that God desires us to be holy. "But as the One who called you is holy, you also are to be holy in all your conduct" (1 Peter 1:15). Then you must make a personal commitment to holiness and renew that commitment daily. Without a sincere personal commitment, you will never become holy. You can also realize the joy that comes to the believer who obediently pursues holiness. So don't be afraid of becoming a holy person.

2. **Decide to study holiness.** While you may desire to study God's Word, you must discipline yourself to do it. So decide if you will complete this Bible study on your own or if you prefer to study with a small group. Personal Bible study is essential to spiritual growth, and shared instruction enhances personal insights. Commit to complete the study you begin. A definite decision to pursue holiness is essential.

3. **Gather resources about holiness.** This Bible study book will be a helpful resource for your study of holiness, but

you can benefit from additional resources, too. Select a Bible translation that you can use confidently or gather several translations to reference. (This Bible study uses the Holman Christian Standard Version unless otherwise noted.) You can refer to the numerous resources listed in the back of this book for additional study. Throughout the centuries, many Christians have written about holiness. You can learn from what God teaches others. You can also find additional resources on your own.

4. **Study and apply the Scripture.** Each lesson will focus on one specific aspect of holiness. Some lessons will focus on a key passage of Scripture while others will examine numerous Scriptures about holiness.

   Read the passages, study their meanings, and apply their truths in your own life. Each lesson encourages personal response and includes Scripture focus (Holy Scripture for Holy Living) plus a section on practical application (Practice Personal Holiness). The selected key Scripture is excellent for Bible memory. Each lesson should take 30 to 45 minutes to complete. As you read each lesson, find each Scripture and answer every question, God will teach you about holiness. Try to complete one lesson in one week over a period of 12 weeks so God can make holiness a part of your everyday life.

5. **Discuss holiness.** This Bible study was designed for individual study, to be completed personally. However, discussion will make the study more meaningful. If you are participating in a small-group study using this material, take advantage of the blessings that come through studying the Scripture with other believers. Anticipate God's work in your life and the life of your group. A group teaching guide is available in the back of the book for small group Bible study. If you are not a part of a group study, then share what God is teaching you with someone else one-on-one.

6. **Share your commitment to holiness.** While it is important for you to share what you learn about holiness with the Lord in prayer and with believers in small group study, it is also challenging to share your commitment to holiness as accountability to believers and as a witness to unbelievers. God wants to use your commitment to holy living to bring glory to Him and bring others to saving faith. So speak freely about your Holy God and His power for holy living.

7. **Continue to be holy.** When you have completed this study of holiness, remember that the process has just begun. You must persevere in your pursuit of holiness in order to live a holy life. God and others will hold you accountable for holiness. And God alone will reward you for righteousness!

8. **Enjoy the blessings of holiness.** Though the holy life is not always an easy life, it is a joyous life. As you follow the example of Christ and obey His teachings, you will receive His blessings. There is no greater joy than the joy of the holy life. Godly Christian women can enjoy the blessings of holiness. May God teach you about Himself and transform you into a godly woman! He can do that if you persevere in your Bible study and in your pursuit of holiness.

Lesson 1
A Holy God

Isaiah 6:3—*"Holy, holy, holy is the LORD of Hosts; His glory fills the whole earth."*

Christians are to be Christlike or little Christs. If that statement is true, then Christians must know what Christ is like. We must not only believe in Christ, we must also pattern our lives after Him. We must know who He is so we can become who He wants us to be. Christ is God in the flesh, sent to provide salvation for our sin. The Bible reveals that God is holy and we are to be holy like Him (1 Peter 1:15–16). The Bible teaches that Christ lived the only sinless, perfect life (Matthew 5:28). So let's examine the Scripture carefully to better understand the holiness of God and the holy, Christlike life He has called us to live.

What Does Holy Mean?

More than any other attribute, the Bible describes the holiness of God. All of His attributes flow out of His holiness. It is completely accurate and totally true to say, "God is holy!" He alone is truly holy.

What does holy tell us about God? In the *Holman Bible Dictionary*, John D. W. Watts suggests three biblical meanings of the word *holy*. Holy means "to be set apart," "to be perfect, transcendent, or spiritually pure," and "to evoke adoration and reverence." In this lesson we will examine all three meanings, but in this study we will use "being set apart for God" as the key meaning. Our God is certainly holy—set apart, perfect, to be adored!

In the Old Testament, the word *holy* (Hebrew word *quadosh*) appears 116 times and literally means "sacred, selected, pure." The very nature of God is pure, thus all of His attributes and actions are pure. He is the Holy One; there is no other like Him. His name is holy and His ways are holy. Because God is holy, He deserves our respect and worship and praise.

The psalmist David proclaimed praises to the Lord for His holiness. In Psalm 99:9, he concluded, *"Exalt the LORD our God; worship at His holy mountain, for the Lord our God is holy."* The Old Testament is filled with references about the holiness of God and His desire for His people to be holy. While the human vocabulary is limited, the psalmist David and others tried to find words to describe the Holy God. We must study Scripture to understand better the indescribable holiness of God. God is holy and holy is God.

In the New Testament, the word *holy* (Greek word *hagios*) literally means "set apart, sanctified, consecrated." While mentioned less often than in the Old Testament, the holiness of God is discussed in the Gospels as well as several New Testament epistles. The work of the Holy Spirit, which is necessary for holiness, is emphasized more in the New Testament than the holy nature of God. The writer of Hebrews clearly affirmed the holiness of God in Hebrews 7:26: *"For this is the kind of high priest we need: holy, innocent, undefiled, separated from sinners, and exalted above the heavens."* The Bible—the Old Testament and New Testament—clearly states that God is holy. Holiness is not what God does, but who He is.

The contemporary world has a distorted view of the word *holy*, which actually comes from the Anglo–Saxon word *halig*, meaning soundness and completeness. Today it frequently relates to health and wellness—physical wholeness. However, the dictionary does include a definition of *holy*: "exalted or worthy of complete devotion as one perfect in goodness and righteousness." God is thought to be holy by most people. He is respected and exalted even by those who do not have personal faith in Him. As the true Holy One, perfect in nature and action, He deserves deep love and devotion from everyone. As we better understand holiness, we can better express our devotion to the Holy One, and we can better develop a holy nature and lifestyle.

The most common understanding of holiness is being set apart. Our Holy God is truly set apart from all others. While many other gods and many religious leaders are good, only the God of the Bible is holy. He alone is fully righteous, which sets Him apart from any other. As His children choose to follow Him, God requires from them a lifestyle of holiness. Before we explore the believer's pursuit of holiness, let's appreciate our Holy God.

Holy—Set Apart

What does the word *holy* mean to you? You have reflected on the understanding of the word and Scripture regarding holiness, but take a few minutes before you continue your study to record your insights.

How do you think the world today perceives the word *holy*?

____

____

____

Now write your own definition of the word *holy*. *Holy* means:

____

____

____

Based on your own definition, do you believe God is holy? If you do, He should receive your devotion and praise as well as your efforts in holy living.

Reflect on what the Scripture teaches about this term. Many biblical scholars say holy means "set apart."

What does it mean to be set apart?

____

____

____

In a conversation with one of my teenage nephews, I challenged him to live a holy life. I tried to explain clearly being set apart, different from the others, and like Christ. My nephew understood the message and got to the bottom line—"You mean we Christians must be weird." Yes, to be set apart does mean to be weird—unlike most others. But remember we are set apart *from* the world and set apart *for* God.

Paul spoke in his writings about being set apart—being in the world but not of the world. Jesus tried to explain this concept of uniqueness to his followers. Read John 15:19 and let Jesus remind you: *"Because you are not of the world, but I have chosen you out of it."*

God clearly conveyed His holiness to the prophet in Isaiah 6:3: *"Holy, holy, holy is the LORD of Hosts; His glory fills the whole earth."* God is like no other. He is different, set apart. The repetition of the word *holy* emphasizes this attribute and elevates the nature of God beyond all others. He is literally "in a class of His own." He is set apart. The repetition of the word *holy* three times reinforces the threefold nature of God as Father, Son, and Holy Spirit (the Trinity). As His children, God makes us holy by setting us apart for Himself. What joy!

Now read that entire passage of Isaiah 6:1–8 and describe the holiness of God in your own terms.

____

____

____

____

____

____

____

Picture God high and lifted up, seated on His throne—separated from all others by His holiness. The seraphim, or the six-winged fiery creatures who guarded God in His temple, proclaimed His holiness to one another. God's royal position and His righteous behavior separated Him then and now from all others.

Do you know someone whose godly life sets her apart from all others? Write her name here and thank the Lord for her godly influence. ________________. What a powerful impact a Christian can have on others! Pray that God will help you be that kind of holy one.

Every believer should grow in grace and strive for sanctification, which is the process of holiness we receive through the grace of God. As she does, her godly life becomes more obvious, more unique in this ungodly world. Throughout history, priests, nuns, and monks have been physically separated from the world so they could be spiritually holy. While God does not call all His children to life in a monastery, He does convict us to be different from the world because of our holy living.

Holy—Without Sin

God is holy because He is set apart from all others. He is also without sin. It is humanly impossible to imagine that anyone could be without sin blameless, perfect, spiritually pure. But the Scripture teaches that God who is holy is sinless—spotless and without blemish (Hebrews 9:14).

What do you think of when you hear the word *sin*?

Circle any of the following phrases that would express your understanding of sin.

Sin is:

a. falling short

b. any act of rebellion

c. selfish behavior

d. getting caught doing the wrong thing

How do these phrases explain the meaning of sin? Ask yourself which is more fun, brings more happiness and joy—sin or righteousness? While sin may give temporary thrills, only righteousness leads to lasting joy. Reflect on the answers then return to the Scripture for true understanding. The Greek word for sin (*hamartia*) literally means "to miss the mark" or fall short of attaining God's standard. Romans 3:23 says, *"For all have sinned and fall short of the glory of God."* Only God is without sin; all others are sinful by nature.

God described His sinless character in His covenant with the psalmist David. If David obeyed His commandments, God promised to be faithful and merciful to him and his descendants. In Psalm 89:30–37, God assured David that He could be trusted because of His holiness.

Read that passage, then fill in the blanks below to describe the sinless character of God.

Verse 33—*"I will not withdraw My ________ ________ from him"*

Verse 33—*"or betray My ________________"*

Verse 34—*"I will not violate My _______________"*

Verse 34—*"or change what My lips ___________ ___________"*

Verse 35—*"I have sworn an oath by My _____________"*

Verse 35—*"I will not _____________ to David"*

God's holiness is reflected in His sinless character and His loving behavior toward us. He promised David, and He promises us that He will not withdraw His faithful love or betray His faithfulness (v. 33). He will never break a covenant, and He will never lie (v. 34). He has sworn an oath on His holiness that He will not lie (v. 35).

Though we are sinful by nature, untruthful and unholy, God alone is all-holy. He can make us holy as we trust in Him and walk in Him. To be holy is to pattern your life after God's righteousness. Our God who is without sin is always holy. You can count on that.

Holy—Evoking Awe

Because God the Holy One is set apart and without sin, He should evoke awe from all believers. We should be filled not only with joy and praise but also with total respect and amazement. He is a mighty Creator and merciful Redeemer.

Ayers Rock in Australia inspires awe. It is one gigantic block of red sandstone jutting up toward the sky in the middle of a vast and empty desert. Its beauty is magnificent. When I visited there, I was drawn to its grandeur. I was left speechless to describe its majesty. In the same way, our eyes should focus on God's creation and His character with reverence and awe. God deserves our sublime adoration because of His perfect holiness as well as His creative power.

Though Moses knew he was weak and inadequate, he asked the Lord to reveal His holiness in a personal way, and God did. When he saw the glory of God, Moses was filled with awe.

Read this account in Exodus 33:12–23, and you will also be in awe of God.

In two distinct ways, Moses asked God to reveal Himself: *"Teach me Your ways"* (v. 13) and *"Please, let me see Your glory"* (v. 18). Desperate for help in leading the Israelites to the Promised Land, Moses cried out to know God's character and His will. God's children today should also call out for Him to teach us His perfect ways and show us His divine glory.

How did God respond to Moses's plea? Read Exodus 33:17 and describe God's response.

____

____

God honored the obedience and faithfulness of Moses by revealing His holiness and promising His presence.

Has God ever revealed Himself to you? Remember that time and record it here.

How did you respond to the Holy One?

Believers should always respond with the awe, devotion, and obedience that our holy God deserves. As we cry out to the Lord in deep love and adoration, He faithfully reveals His perfect holiness.

God has revealed Himself to me in many awe-inspiring ways through His character and His creation. His pure, sinless, blameless, nature sets Him apart from all others and earns my praise. His holy nature deserves even more accolades than His beautiful creation.

Some years ago, my husband and I traveled to Africa and visited Victoria Falls in Zimbabwe. Far in the distance, we could see the mist from the massive waterfalls. Then we explored the one-and-a-half mile long waterfall discovered in the mid-nineteenth century by missionary David Livingstone. At each stop the view became more spectacular—a curtain of falling water, the winding gorge below, rainbows overhead, the thunderous roar of the water. As we rounded the last bend, we were amazed to see two complete rainbows. The sights and sounds reminded us of the power of our God. We were speechless as we observed this wonder of the world, and we were in awe as God revealed Himself to us.

As you reflect on times God has shown His glory and holiness to you, sing the chorus of praise, "Our God Is an Awesome God." God is truly awesome not just in creation but in our lives.

It is essential to remember that God is holy—He is the Holy One. The Bible teaches about the holiness of a perfect God who is separate and apart from others, who is totally without sin. It challenges us to respond to the holiness of God with reverence and devotion.

While we will not achieve perfect holiness this side of heaven, believers are to imitate the character and conduct of the Holy One. Holiness is to be desired and not feared. It will bring a sense of wonder into your life. So embrace holiness with eager anticipation. In the next lesson, we will examine our own natures as we learn to become a holy people.

Holy Scripture for Holy Living

Write the Scripture verse at the beginning of the chapter in the space provided below then try to memorize it this week.

Practice Personal Holiness

Are you consciously aware of the holiness of God? List three ways that God reveals His holiness to you.

1. ______________________________

2. ______________________________

3. ______________________________

Reflect on God who is set apart and without sin. Record below a prayer of praise to the Holy One, expressing your awe and reverence.

____

____

____

____

____

Lesson 2
A Holy People

1 Peter 1:15–16—*"As the One who called you is holy, you also are to be holy in all your conduct; for it is written, 'Be holy, because I am holy.' "*

Christians are not surprised to learn of the holiness of God. Because we believe He is the Almighty Creator and Sovereign Ruler, we trust Him to be holy. We are confident that He is set apart from all others and completely without sin. His holiness brings awe and reverence to the hearts of believers and amazement even to those who do not believe personally. However, believers are challenged when God in His Word calls us to be holy like Him. Holiness seems natural for God but totally impossible for people. God, who created us in His image (Genesis 1:27), desires us to be like Him—holy, righteous, godly.

A Command for Holiness

Before we seek help in living a holy life, let's examine the biblical commands for personal holiness. As quickly as He confirms His own holiness, God challenges His children to be holy. It is innate for a father to desire only the best from his children. Thus, God wants His children to be holy and intends for holiness to be a blessing, not a burden. God our heavenly Father not only desires our holiness, He commands us to be holy and empowers us to be holy.

In 1 Peter 1:13–21, the Lord, who breathed the words of Scripture, mandates us to be holy.

Read this passage as an introduction to this lesson. Notice Peter's description of holy behavior and his assurance of God's power to give us hope and holiness.

First Peter 1:16 is the focal passage: "It is written, be holy, because I am holy." Peter learned this teaching personally from Jesus in the Sermon on the Mount (Matthew 5:48). Jesus clearly stated that believers are to be holy in their natures, just as God is holy.

Look back at 1 Peter 1:15–16 to see how many times the word *holy* is used. Write that number here. ______

The word *holy* is written by the disciple Peter four times in this brief Scripture passage. Two times the word is used to describe God—*"the One who called you is holy"* (v. 15) and *"I am holy"* (v. 16). Twice the writer uses the word *holy* as a challenge to godly living—*"be holy in all your conduct"* (v. 15) and *"be holy"* (v. 16). It is clear from Scripture that the believer should seek to be holy like God. In other words, we are to act like we belong to God. He set us apart for Himself.

As a teenager growing up in the city of New Orleans, I was confronted daily by God's command for holiness, while my friends and others around me lived life on their own terms. As a believer, I was challenged to be like my Holy God. I didn't always like God's command, and I didn't always follow His command, but when I did, I knew I was a reflection of His righteousness in the world.

Recently I visited with an old high school friend. Though she often had teased me about my "holier than thou" behavior, I knew she also respected me. My friend has come to know the Lord. I was humbled when she told me that I was the only person she knew while we were growing up that actually lived like the Christian she was supposed to be. How grateful I am that I followed God's command for holiness! For it is true, we are the only Jesus many people will ever see!

A Call to Holiness

Knowing that God loves *you* is a humbling thought. His love and mercy are personal. He offers salvation by faith to all, and His offer is extended to you and me. God's provision and power are also personal. He knows your needs and meets them in His time. In addition, God desires each one of His children to be holy. It is not enough for *some* to be holy. His heart's desire is for *all* His children to be holy. His call to holiness is personal and persistent.

A holy God has called you to be holy (1 Peter 1:15). You embraced His call to holiness at the time of your conversion and that call will continue throughout your lifetime. A *call* is an invitation from God to respond as He directs. God calls all to salvation and all believers to holy living.

Read the following Scriptures and note a biblical teaching about God's call.

2 Thessalonians 2:13–15 ________________________________

1 Corinthians 1:9 ________________________________

2 Timothy 1:9 ________________________________

Hebrews 9:15 ________________________________

1 Peter 1:15 ________________________________

God has called you to salvation (2 Thessalonians 2:13–15) and to fellowship with Him (1 Corinthians 1:9). He calls you to serve Him (2 Timothy 1:9) and to receive an eternal inheritance (Hebrews 9:15). God's call is personal and specific; He calls all believers to be a holy people (1 Peter 1:15).

Take a minute to reflect back on God's call in your own life. Record a brief testimony of God's call to salvation, service, and sanctification (holiness).

My call to salvation (conversion): ________________________

____

____

____

My call to service (ministry):

My call to sanctification (holiness):

Thank God for His call in your life—His personal invitation to salvation, service, and sanctification! I thank God for His call in my own life. At the young age of six and half years, I accepted God's call to salvation. It was a personal call from God, not from my parents or a Christian friend. As a teenager, I accepted God's call to service. Though I didn't know exactly how I would serve, I knew God had a special ministry for me. My call to sanctification, which began at the time of my conversion, was renewed a few years ago when several friends failed in their personal lives. His call is ongoing in my life, God calls me daily to holiness!

A Conduct of Holiness

God clearly commands His children to live holy lives and calls us to be holy like Him. His Word then gives practical instruction—a code of holiness. Specific behavior reflects a holy character. Christians are to conduct themselves in a different way than the world. We are to *be* holy and *live* holy.

The biblical term for the process of being made holy is *sanctification*. Sanctification begins at the time of conversion and continues throughout life as the believer seeks to be more Christlike. It is essential for you to understand thoroughly this important biblical concept. Let's consider three theological words that describe the experience of salvation.

Justification is the process of beginning a personal relationship with Christ through faith. Through justification, an individual is saved from the **penalty** of sin (Romans 6:23). *Sanctification* is the process of being made holy like Him. In sanctification, the believer is saved from the **power** of sin (1 Corinthians 10:13). *Glorification* is the process of becoming completely like Him when the believer is saved from the **presence** of sin (2 Corinthians 3:18). Glorification comes to the believer only when you are with the Father in heaven for all eternity.

Do you understand these three important terms? If not, reread their explanations. Then try to explain them simply to a friend or write them here in your own words.

Justification— ______________________________

____

____

____

Sanctification— ______________________________

____

____

____

____

Glorification– ______________________________________

____

____

____

The Old Testament talks about the sanctified life—a holy lifestyle. In the Book of Leviticus many laws or guidelines are given by a holy God to promote holy living among His children. The original Ten Commandments given by God to Moses on Mount Sinai are often explained and expanded in Scripture. In Leviticus 19:1–2, *"The LORD spoke to Moses: 'Speak to the entire community and tell them: Be holy because I, the LORD your God, am holy.'"* The Lord then clarified His commands.

Read Leviticus 19 and list below ten specific guidelines for holy conduct.

1. ____

2. ____

3. ____

4. ____

5. ____

6. ____

7. ______________________________

8. ______________________________

9. ______________________________

10. ______________________________

Like the Ten Commandments, these guidelines in Leviticus 19 direct our relationship with God and others. Believers should worship only God, keep the Sabbath, give offerings sacrificially, and obey His commandments. We should not take His name in vain nor harm His godly witness with our ungodly behavior.

Leviticus 19 instructs us to be holy in our relationships with others. We should honor our parents, care for the needy, be just and loving, and treat all people with respect. We should not steal from others nor lie. We should avoid hate and sexual immorality. We should honor God with our hearts and our lifestyles, not profane Him with our words or actions.

Each summer the campus of New Orleans Baptist Theological Seminary fills with teenagers who are a part of our Mission Lab program. They come from around the country to spend a week ministering in our city. These young volunteers work in community centers, on construction projects, with homeless people, and in many other meaningful endeavors. The city and the students are changed by this sacrificial service.

I attended the opening worship service for the Mission Lab this summer. It was a dynamic time of praise and proclamation with those energetic youth. Each of us was challenged to "be the church." At the end of the service, a very creative video was shown to challenge the teens to behave like Christ while serving others in His name. The "Follow the Rules" rap not only outlined the program expectations in a humorous way, but it clearly established a code of holy conduct for believers on mission. We all need to be reminded that God's guidelines for holiness are always to be followed. A call to holiness leads to a conduct of holiness, but neither the call nor the conduct will develop without a personal commitment.

A Commitment to Holiness

Holiness begins with the invitation by God to be holy as He is holy. Then each believer must make a personal response. Commitment demands a choice of the heart and change in behavior. Thus when a believer makes a commitment to the Lord, a lifestyle change must take place—holiness. We are to strive to *"be perfect, therefore, as your heavenly Father is perfect"* (Matthew 5:48).

Jesus Himself made a personal commitment to His Father. He determined to do God's will, not His own, even when it meant death. In the Garden of Gethsemane, Jesus made a profound commitment: *"Not as I will, but as You will"* (Matthew 26:39). The Son of God was not exempt from making a personal commitment to His Heavenly Father. Believers are to commit to God's will—total surrender and true holiness.

As a Christian teenager growing up in a sinful city like New Orleans, I had to make a personal commitment to holiness. It wasn't enough for my parents to be godly or my friends to be Christlike. I had to make my own decision to be holy like my God. I remember that turning point in my own life when I decided to follow the holy lifestyle of Jesus, not the unholy lifestyles of those around me. That commitment made a difference in my conduct. I am grateful for my "boring testimony"—a life that was not tarnished by unrighteous behavior and deliberate rebellion. Since that time, I have made many personal recommitments to holiness. Surrounded by unholiness in the world, every believer must continually commit to live like Christ each and every day.

In calling His disciples, Jesus demanded a commitment. He extended the personal invitation, but expected an individual response.

Turn in your Bible to Matthew 4:18–22, and read the call of Jesus to four disciples.

What was His call? ______________________________

How did they respond? ______________________________

____

How do you respond to the call of Jesus? ______________________

____

____

____

Jesus clearly commanded that the fishermen follow Him, and they responded obediently without hesitation. When the disciples followed, Jesus made them fishers of men. My husband, Chuck, preaches a powerful sermon from this passage. He clearly explains the initial command of Jesus in Matthew 4:19—*"follow me."* Then Chuck identifies the eventual result—*"you will be fishers of men."* However, he is quick to point out the power in the middle—*"I will make you."* Jesus doesn't call us to commit to holiness and leave us to figure it out on our own. He promises to make us like Him—holy, to make us fishers of men. He gives us a command with a promise!

Jesus demanded a commitment from another person in Scripture—the adulterous woman. The Apostle John recorded the encounter of Jesus with the woman caught in adultery (John 8:2–11). When the scribes and the Pharisees demanded a verdict from Jesus, He spoke personally to the woman, offering forgiveness of her sin. Then He commanded her to commit to holy living—*"go, and from now on do not sin any more"* (John 8:11).

The adulterous woman received a call to holiness, which included a conduct of holiness as a result of a commitment to holiness. Have you made a similar commitment? God's holiness is without question. Our holiness should be a natural response of love and obedience. Our answer should be yes as we commit ourselves to holy living. God who is holy can make you holy too!

Holy Scripture for Holy Living

Write the Scripture verse at the beginning of the chapter here. Then try to memorize it this week.

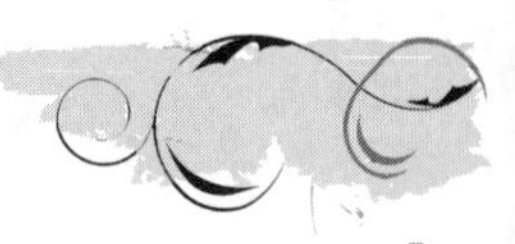

Practice Personal Holiness

Remember that you do not become holy on your own. God's working in and through you brings holiness. In the space below, record a commitment to holiness. Discuss your call to holy living and your plan for accomplishing that goal. Then sign the commitment at the bottom.

____

____

____

____

____

____

____

____

____

____

Signature ______________________________ Date ______________

Lesson 3
A Life of Holiness

1 Thessalonians 4:7 (NKJV) – *"For God did not call us to uncleanness, but in holiness."*

Young children often fantasize about what they want to be when they grow up—a teacher, a doctor, a nurse, a mommy. They have natural interests and desires. As we grow up, even as adults, we envision our lives as we hope they will be.

As a child, I always wanted to be a helper. I was my mommy's helper and often pretended to be a nurse or a teacher helping other people. As a teenager, my personal aspirations became more specific. I knew I loved to talk and wanted to help others talk since communication is so important to all human beings. So I began to explore the field of speech pathology. I completed my education preparing me for that profession then began working in the medical field in the area of communicative disorders. Speech pathology was my career in life, but ministry to people was my spiritual calling. Today God has focused my life on ministry to women—my lifelong calling.

God gives His children aspirations and professional pursuits, but He gives each child one clear goal for living—a life of holiness. Holy living is not natural behavior for a child. We are born sinful in our very natures. If you doubt that statement, watch a young child who defies authority and seeks personal desires. Those selfish desires continue to control us into adulthood. Thus God desires all believers to be different—to live a holy life. In the same way that all children must grow up physically and mentally, Christians must grow up spiritually. We must grow up into holiness. Again, let's turn to the Scripture for a biblical perspective on this life of holiness.

Holiness Is a Higher Calling from God

The Apostle Paul ministered in a time of great ungodliness. There were no people more ungodly than the Thessalonians, whose sexual immorality was legendary. In that atmosphere of promiscuity, Paul wrote his letter to the Christians in Thessalonica challenging them to be different—to be holy in an unholy world. Paul reminded the early Christians that God's call to believers was for holiness not uncleanliness. The call of God to Christians today is the same. It is a higher call—a call to live a pure and holy life.

Read 1 Thessalonians 4:1–8. Underline key words or phrases that explain God's high call to holy living. What do you understand the Scripture to mean when Paul says each of the following commands?

"*walk*" (v. 1) ____________________

____

____

____

"*please God*" (v. 1)____________________

____

____

____

"*do so even more*" (v. 1)____________________

____

____

____

"possess [your] own vessel in sanctification and honor" (v. 4)_______

____

____

____

God extends to believers a higher calling to live a holy life. Salvation offers more than a guarantee of eternal security. My husband says that "salvation is more than a fire insurance policy and pew sores." It should bring about a change in lifestyle as well as eternal life. Paul said we are to *"do so even more"* in righteousness after our conversion (1 Thessalonians 4:1). Believers are to *continue* becoming holy—living not in your own power but in the power of the Holy Spirit. With the help of God's Spirit, believers can uphold God's higher calling to sanctified living.

How are you doing in fulfilling your high calling to holiness? Using the exact phrases from Scripture, rate yourself on a scale from 1 to 10, with 1 being the lowest score and 10 being the highest. Evaluate your own response to God's high call to holiness.

"walk" (v. 1) ___________________________________

____

____

____

"please God" (v. 1) ______________________________

____

____

____

"do so even more" (v. 1) ______________________________

____

____

____

"possess [your] *own vessel in sanctification and honor"* (v. 4) ______

____

____

____

Though often considered politically incorrect, beauty pageants still recognize women for their outer beauty as well as their inner character. Winners of these competitions earn recognition and rewards, but they also assume responsibilities. They must rise up to a higher standard of behavior as they represent themselves, their positions, and the organizations. Through the years, beauty queens have lost their crowns due to behavior unbecoming of their position. Their reigns have been cut short because of low standards of living. When individuals accept Christ, they receive the rewards of salvation, but we also accept the responsibilities. Holiness is a heavy responsibility of salvation.

It is always sobering to realize how far every person falls short of the glory of God. Failures happen among Christians and ministers just as they happen to beauty queens. You and I fall short in holiness because we are sinful creatures. But don't spend too much time focusing on your failures. Recommit your life to the high calling of holy living.

Paul also spoke to the Christians in Philippi about holiness. He told them to keep pressing on in their spiritual growth. As believers forget the failures of the past and look ahead to a renewed walk with the Lord, holy lifestyles can be achieved. The goal is then accomplished and the prize is won: *"God's heavenly call in Christ Jesus"* (Philippians 3:12–14).

Holiness Is the Will of God

Once a believer understands God's call to a life of holiness, she often struggles with knowing and doing the will of God. While God's will does affect your vocation and daily choices, it also impacts your lifestyle. You may be unsure of the specific occupation or path God has chosen for you. But, you should understand without a doubt that God wants you to live a holy life. A godly lifestyle should set all Christians apart from the world.

Paul reminded the Thessalonian Christians that God's will is for His children to be sanctified and holy.

Turn again to 1 Thessalonians 4 and reread verses 3 through 6.

What is God's will for your life? ______________________________

____

____

____

State that in the following sentence by filling your own name in the blank.

> ***"For this is God's will, _________________'s sanctification"* (1 Thessalonians 4:3).**

If we will focus more on living a holy life, then God will reveal His plan and purpose in His time.

Generally speaking, God's will for all His children is to be holy. Specifically, holiness is lived out in different ways in individual lives. In another New Testament epistle, the Apostle Paul gives specific instructions for Christians to do God's will.

Read the familiar passage in Romans 12:1–2 and paraphrase that passage below in your own words.

____

____

____

____

____

Paul understood God's perfect will to be good, holy, and pleasing—a lifestyle different from the world. He passionately pleaded with the believers not to act like unbelievers, since God had done so much for them. In gratitude, God's children should live consecrated, righteous lives. Each believer is to make a personal sacrifice of self in order to be sanctified and serve the Savior.

In her book, *The Christian's Secret of a Happy Life,* Hannah Whitall Smith sadly acknowledges the sinful lives of Christians in the late eighteenth—nineteenth century. "The standard of practical holy living has been so low among Christians that the least degree of real devotedness of life and walk is looked upon with surprise... by a large portion of the Church. And, for the most part, the followers of Jesus Christ are satisfied with a life so conformed to the world, and so like it in almost every respect, that, to a casual observer, no difference is discernible." Unfortunately, her conclusion is true today in the early twenty-first century. The lives of Christians are so much like the world that unbelievers cannot tell the difference.

While the world has influenced the church toward sinfulness, and the devil attempts to mold you into his sinful image, God wants to transform you into His holy image. It is God's will for His children to be counter-cultural, to impact the world with their holy living.

What are some of the temptations you face in the world? List a few ways the world has tried to conform you:

1. ____

2. ____

3. ____

Now ask God's forgiveness and recommit yourself to holiness, which is the perfect will of God.

Holiness Is Pleasing to God

Sanctified living is the highest call of God and the perfect will of God. Our holy living also pleases God more than anything else we could say or do. It is tempting to think that our Christian service or our productive ministry is most pleasing to God. That is not true. A godly life is the greatest tribute to God.

My Christian parents express true joy when my life is committed to the Lord, and I am serving Him. My husband's parents are proud of their son, Chuck Kelley, and son-in-law, Paige Patterson, who are influential Christian leaders. Christian parents often pray diligently that their children will be involved in Christian ministry, but they must pray that their children will stay close to the Lord and rejoice when they live for Him faithfully. The joy of parents over the godly lives of their children is only a hint of God's pleasure when His children live holy lives.

Read the following Scriptures and identify what behavior pleases God.

Philippians 4:18 ______________________________________

Colossians 3:20 ______________________________________

Hebrews 13:21 ______________________________________

Paul received gifts from his Christian friends in Philippi—their generosity was *"a fragrant offering, a welcome sacrifice, pleasing to God"* (Philippians 4:18). God must truly rejoice when we live our lives for others. In another letter, Paul acknowledged that obedience to God's plan for relationships is *"pleasing to the Lord"* (Colossians 3:20). When we submit, love, and obey, God is pleased with our lives. In a later New Testament letter, the writer of Hebrews said he works in us *"what is pleasing in His sight"* (Hebrews 13:21). A lifetime of holiness brings God our Father great pleasure.

What pleases you? While some material things or personal experiences may make you happy, true pleasure comes through expressions of love by other people. A wife is most pleased when her husband says "I love you" with or without an expensive present. A mother experiences true joy in the enthusiastic hug of her child. A friend finds pleasure in the unconditional love of another.

God is pleased when His children love Him and live for Him. A holy life pleases Him the most. A holy life demonstrates itself through unselfish generosity and faithful obedience. While good works are not the basis for a relationship with God, good works should flow from a relationship with God. Christians should respond to God's call to a life of holiness because it is His highest calling, His divine will, and His deepest pleasure.

Holy Scripture for Holy Living

Write the Scripture verse at the beginning of the chapter here. Then try to memorize it this week.

____

____

____

____

____

____

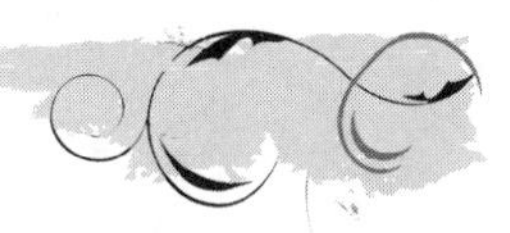

Practice Personal Holiness

What have you done recently that you believe truly pleased the Lord? Write that achievement below and explain why you believe God was pleased. ______________________________

____

____

____

____

____

____

Make a renewed commitment to please God through your holy living. ______________________________

____

____

____

____

____

____

Lesson 4
Holy Heroes

Luke 1:6—[Elizabeth was] *"righteous in God's sight, living without blame according to all the commandments and requirements of the Lord."*

Throughout time, people have looked to other people for inspiration and encouragement. Our human nature is to place individuals who have excelled or succeeded in life on a pedestal, in a position of honor; they become role models to respect and imitate. Though personal rights and individuality are promoted, we naturally look to others as real-life examples. Young or old, we have heroes.

A ten-year-old "boy wonder" named Gregory Smith recently gave his high school commencement address and challenged the graduates to imitate his heroes. His goal in life he said was to get three PhDs so he could help change the world and eliminate violence. He passionately called his much older classmates to promote peace and love their enemies. He encouraged them to model their lives after his heroes: Martin Luther King, Mahatma Gandhi, and Jesus Christ. Though many people may marvel at this whiz kid, he desires to emulate those he sees as truly great. This hero has heroes.

Who is your hero? Who are some people you look up to because of their character and contributions? Christians need holy heroes who model the holiness of God. The Bible is filled with stories about holy heroes. History includes the accounts of holy heroes. Even today Christians can look up to modern holy heroes. These godly individuals are examples for us to learn from and role models for us to imitate.

Let's examine a few holy heroes in the Bible and others from more recent history. As you learn about them, think of women who have been role models for you in Christian living. Ask God to help you be a holy hero in an unholy world.

Though the Old and New Testaments are filled with examples of holy heroes, let's look in one of the Gospels at the lives of three godly women. Turn to the Book of Luke and read about these heroines of holiness. Can you determine what characteristics and actions make them holy heroes? Each serves distinctly as a role model for a specific reason. If you imitate their holiness, you can be a holy hero too.

Heroic Righteousness

First, turn to Luke 1. Elizabeth, the wife of Zechariah and mother of John the Baptist, was an example for Mary, the mother of Jesus, and all Christian women because of her righteousness. She had a strong faith that was lived out in her daily life.

Read Luke 1:5–6 and determine why Elizabeth was found to be righteous before God. Record your ideas here.

____

____

____

____

Luke describes Elizabeth as righteous before God because she lived *"without blame according to all the commandments and requirements of the Lord"* (Luke 1:6). Since she obeyed the Lord and lived a pure life, Elizabeth was a holy hero. She was determined to live by the law and follow all of its ordinances. Because of her holiness, she influenced the mother of Jesus to accept the Lord's plan and give birth to the Savior of the world.

I know a contemporary heroine who desires to be found righteous before God. Her name is Iris Blue, and her testimony is powerful. She was drawn to the Lord as a prostitute and a convict because all she wanted was to be a lady. While in jail, this ungodly woman says she "knelt down a tramp and stood up a lady" as God saved her from her sin and made her holy like Him. What an example of

God's mercy and grace. God used Iris as a dynamic witness in her ungodly world, and now He uses her to challenge Christians everywhere to be holy. He can transform the unholy into holy and make each life a witness of heroic righteousness.

Heroic Service

Luke's Gospel includes the account of another holy hero. Anna, a widow of great age, served the Lord faithfully in the temple alongside Simeon, one who was "righteous and devout" (Luke 2:25). When Jesus entered the temple with His parents, Anna recognized Jesus as the promised Messiah. She was chosen to see the Redeemer because of her faithfulness and service. She was a holy hero who challenges us to *"live in a sensible, righteous, and godly way in the present age, while we wait for the blessed hope and the appearing of the glory of our great God and Savior, Jesus Christ"* (Titus 2:12–13).

Turn in your Bible to the story of Anna in Luke 2:36–38. After you read this Scripture passage, write a brief description of Anna.

____

____

____

____

____

____

Luke describes Anna's words and actions, as well as her character. She spoke with confidence, proclaiming the birth of the Messiah, and she served God faithfully. God spoke through her and she spoke of Him. Anna *"served God night and day with fastings and prayers"* (Luke 2:37). Her service was sacrificial and continual. She was respected and praised for her heroic service. She is a holy hero who deserves our recognition and emulation.

At the turn of the twentieth century, a missionary in China served sacrificially and continually. Called to proclaim Jesus Christ to the Chinese people, Lottie Moon served them unselfishly, giving all that she had to those people who had nothing. She worked with them faithfully for many years. At age 72, she died of starvation so that her Chinese friends could have food. My own mother wrote this note in 1980 in my copy of The New Lottie Moon Story, encouraging me to model my life after the heroic service of Lottie Moon:

> *"My prayer is that you will emulate Christ Jesus who was glorified through Lottie Moon. May the power of the Holy Spirit lead you as you bless many lives!"*

My own mother is a contemporary heroine of service. Like Anna, she is a senior saint who gives her life daily to serving the Lord. She works regularly in our community mission centers, volunteers as a greeter for church conferences, delivers refreshments during Vacation Bible School, bakes her delicious pound cake for neighbors, takes her friends to doctors appointments, and cares for others in many different ways. My husband often says about my mother, "She has retired well—serving the Lord and others every day of her life." What an example of heroic service!

The examples of Anna, a devoted servant in the New Testament, and Lottie Moon, a committed missionary to China, challenge us to heroic service. Luke also included an example of heroic commitment in his Gospel.

Heroic Commitment

Another heroine is described by Luke. She also lived and ministered during the time of Jesus. She was an example of godliness in the time of the early church and continues to be a model of righteousness for Christian women today. Let's learn about the heroic commitment of Mary who lived in Bethany.

In Luke 10, you meet Mary of Bethany and her sister Martha. Read Luke 10:38–42. It is a familiar account that connects you immediately with one personality. Which of these sisters do you identify with and why?

This account describes Mary as sitting at the feet of Jesus and Martha as serving the guests. It is easy to recognize the efforts of Martha without respecting the devotion of Mary. In fact, Christian women today find it much easier to stay busy serving others than to sit quietly and hear from the Lord. Mary teaches us commitment to the better way.

Growing up in a home with only one sibling—a sister—I often related personally to the biblical story of Mary and Martha. My younger sister, Mitzi, and I were just as different as Mary and Martha. We not only look different from each other but we act differently. I always identified with Martha—busy serving and helping in the kitchen while my sister was never in the kitchen; instead, she was sitting in the den talking to our guests. What a reminder to me of proper priorities in life!

Jesus affirmed the commitment of Mary when He said, *"Mary has made the right choice, and it will not be taken away from her"* (Luke 10:42). In this encounter with Jesus, Mary of Bethany demonstrated her devotion to Him. More than serving others, Mary wanted to spend time with Jesus. In other Gospel accounts, Mary's commitment to the Lord is also recorded.

Read the following passages and describe Mary's heroic commitment.

John 11:17–44 ____

____

____

John 12:1–8 ____

____

____

Mary of Bethany has lived throughout history as an example of godly commitment. When the Lord visited her home, she gave Him her undivided attention (Luke 10:39). When her brother Lazarus died, her faith in the Lord did not waver. She expressed confidence in His miraculous power when she said, *"Lord, if you had been here, my brother would not have died"* (John 11:32). And Jesus demonstrated His power when He raised Lazarus from the dead.

In a later encounter, Mary's devotion prompted her to anoint the feet of Jesus with a costly oil (John 12:1–8). Her sacrificial act of commitment gave Jesus the opportunity to teach His disciples about His approaching death on the Cross. The Gospel of Matthew records the praise of Jesus for Mary's heroic commitment: *"'I assure you: Wherever this gospel is proclaimed in the whole world, what this woman has done will also be told in memory of her'"* (Matthew 26:13). Christian women today should strive to be committed to Jesus Christ like Mary—always sitting at His feet.

Though commitment is not a common quality in people today, devotion to the Lord has characterized some contemporary women. One committed woman of faith lived in Holland during World War II. Her name was Corrie ten Boom. *The Hiding Place* tells her story of a family's commitment to protecting Jews from the German Gestapo. After Corrie ten Boom was discovered by the Nazis, she spent almost one year in a concentration camp. During her time of persecution, she clung to her faith for survival. "Lord Jesus, protect me!" was the plea she recorded in her journal. Her commitment never faltered though she lost her parents and her sister, Betsie. During her imprisonment and for the rest of her life, Corrie ten Boom's extraordinary commitment and devotion to God resonated in her words of testimony. Her commitment was heroic when she was confronted to share the gospel with a German soldier who had tortured her. She wrote:

> *"Jesus Christ had died for this man; was I going to ask for more? Lord Jesus, I prayed, forgive me and help me to forgive him. And so I discovered that it is not on our forgiveness any more than our goodness that the world's healing hinges, but on His. When He tells us to love our enemies, He gives, along with the command, the love itself."*

Today there are many living testimonies of commitment—missionaries who serve the Lord all round the world. One precious woman comes to mind immediately. Serving with her husband and five daughters in modern China, Ann's commitment to the Lord did not falter when her husband was killed by a man he was teaching. Though she and her daughters came back to the States briefly, Ann was determined to return with her children to China where God had called them. She reached out in forgiveness to her husband's killer, comforted Chinese friends who were devastated by the tragedy, and cared for her family though she was across the world from home. Ann's heroic commitment to the Lord continues to be a powerful witness!

Many women of the Bible provide examples of godliness for us today. If you haven't read lately about the lives of some holy heroines in the Bible, I encourage you to do so. My Bible study entitled *Life Lessons from Women in the Bible* could be a helpful guide to you as you search the Scripture for godly role models. You should also notice holy heroines living in your world. Read the biographies of missionaries and listen for real-life testimonies of faith. They can encourage you in your journey of holiness and motivate you to be an example of holiness to others.

Holy Scripture for Holy Living

Write the Scripture verse at the beginning of the chapter here. Then try to memorize it this week.

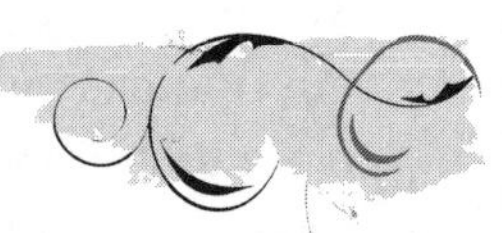

Practice Personal Holiness

Whom do you look up to as a holy hero? Identify that individual and describe why in the space below.

Spend some time in prayer reflecting on the powerful influence you, as a woman living in holiness, can have. Consider your own level of righteousness, service, and commitment before God. Aspire with God to reach your full potential as a holy hero.

Lesson 5
Developing Holiness

Colossians 3:12—*"Therefore, God's chosen ones, holy and loved, put on heartfelt compassion, kindness, humility, gentleness, and patience."*

How does a Christian develop holiness? What a challenging question! It is a question that Christians must ask and attempt to answer. Even more difficult than beginning to live a holy life is continuing to be holy.

Before we specifically identify holy habits, let's discuss the development of holiness in the lives of Christians. The best answer to the "how" question comes from a key word in the definition of the biblical term *sanctification*. According to the *Holman Bible Dictionary*, *sanctification* is "the process of being made holy resulting in a changed lifestyle for the believer." The key word is *process*. Developing holiness is the process of becoming like Christ. It is this ongoing process in the believer's life from salvation to grave that results in a lifestyle of holiness.

The dictionary defines *process* as "something going on" or "a natural phenomenon marked by gradual changes that lead toward a particular result." Several things about a process are clear in these definitions. (1) A process is active and it takes time; (2) a process is gradual; and (3) a process results in change. Holy living is truly a process—gradual steps of faith over time that result in a changed life.

In his letter to the Christians in Colossae, the Apostle Paul talked about the process of sanctification. He challenged believers to *"put off the old man"* and be renewed in the image of God (Colossians 3:9–10). In the third chapter of this epistle, Paul used several words that explain the ongoing process in sanctification. He repeated his theme of developing holiness several times in this brief passage.

Read Colossians 3:1–14 and underline key words or phrases that describe the process of sanctification. Now list below several descriptors of this process.

____

____

____

____

____

This passage thoroughly discusses the process of sanctification in clear and relevant terms. Several phrases express how believers are to become sanctified: *"seek what is above"* (v. 1), *"set your minds on what is above"* (v. 2), *"you have died [to sin]"* (v. 3), *"your life is hidden with the Messiah"* (v. 3), *"put to death whatever in you is worldly"* (v. 5), *"put away all sin"* (v. 8), and *"put on the image of the Creator"* (v. 10). You should have identified some of these key phrases in the space above. Paul understood what was necessary for developing holiness.

In this passage, Paul identified at least three steps in the process of sanctification. If you are to develop holiness you must:

1. Put sin to death—die to your old sinful self.

2. Take off ungodliness—no longer live in sin.

3. Put on godliness—live now in righteousness.

From the point of a person's conversion until the time of her death, God is making His holiness complete in every believer. Now let's carefully examine this process of holiness in Colossians 3.

Put Sin to Death

After Paul exhorted Christians to *"seek what is above"* and *"set your mind on what is above"* (Colossians 3:1–2), he told us how to do it. The first step is "put sin to death." Colossians 3:5 says, *"Therefore put to death whatever in you is worldly."* The phrase translated "put to death" actually comes from the Greek word *nekron*, which means to "reckon as dead." Paul was not actually calling Christians to commit suicide or kill themselves. Instead, he explained that the process of sanctification requires extinguishing evil desires and actions.

What are some of the sinful behaviors that Paul said the believer is to put to death? Reread Colossians 3:5. Then list some of the sins that should no longer be a part of the believer's life.

____

____

____

____

Paul reminded the believer that sexual immorality, impurity, lust, evil desire, greed, and idolatry are sinful behaviors that should no longer be a part of the believer's life. Remember, too, this list of carnal behaviors is not exhaustive. (See Galatians 5:19–21 for example.) In other passages, Paul listed behaviors that are even more sinful. All sin is to be put to death after salvation. We are to die daily to sin.

God sees all sexual immorality as sin that is not compatible with a sanctified life. When an individual commits to holiness, ungodly behaviors should no longer exist. The sinful old self is put to death so a new sinless self can develop. While all sexual sin holds a firm grip on people, homosexuality is particularly tenacious.

In a recent testimony, a beautiful young woman told of the power of homosexual tendencies in her life since her early teens. When she came to salvation and studied the Scripture, she knew she must leave the sinful lifestyle. It was hard—she fought the battle of letting go daily. She had to leave old friends and avoid tempting places, but gradually the Holy Spirit helped her control the power of that sin in her life. She concluded her heart-wrenching testimony by saying, "Every day I must put my old sexual sin to death—I must literally destroy my fleshly desires. And, I know I am fighting a lifelong battle."

Do you understand the practical application in this biblical teaching about the process of sanctification? To develop holiness, a believer must strive to eliminate all ungodliness—all sinful thoughts or behaviors—through the power of the Holy Spirit. When sin is put to death, it no longer exists. Once this is done, holy habits can be developed.

Take Off Ungodliness

Paul added another step to this process of sanctification. After you put sin to death in your life, you must keep on taking off ungodliness. In Colossians 3:8–9, Paul strongly reminded Christians to put off all these things. The process of sanctification continues after the believer extinguishes sinful behavior because sinfulness keeps returning. The believer must daily take off ungodliness. The phrase "put off" or "take off" is associated with the everyday task of dressing, when clothing articles are taken off and put on by the wearer.

Paul reminded Christians that the believer must personally take off ungodliness. Colossians 3:8 says that you *must* do it. This is a command for you alone. It would be so much easier if someone else could do this hard work for us. But the believer herself is responsible for removing sinfulness from her life. Each of us will be held accountable by God for the sinfulness of our own lives.

What ungodly behaviors must the believer take off in order to be holy? Read Colossians 3:8–9. Then list below each act of ungodliness that Paul said to take off. Beside each ungodly behavior, list a personal example of that unholy behavior.

Sin	Example
1. ____________	______________________________
2. ____________	______________________________
3. ____________	______________________________

4. ____________ ____

5. ____________ ____

6. ____________ ____

Now ask God to forgive you of your sin. "Put off" that ungodliness in your life.

Paul cited specific sins of the Christians in Colossae in this passage. Many of those same sins continue to be a problem for Christians today. We must keep on extinguishing or removing from our life these sins of the spirit and the body. Paul listed these sins of the body: sexual sin, immorality, impurity, lust, evil desire, greed, and idolatry. These sins of the flesh result from an ungodly spirit, but sin often begins in the heart with ungodly thoughts and feelings. Ask God to help you control your own unholy behaviors.

Each year at Mardi Gras, the city of New Orleans is filled with people who are flaunting sexual immorality, impurity, and lust. It is a time of moral decadence. While this heathen celebration promotes sinful behavior, surely this sinfulness is present throughout the year. Even those sinners realize that what they are doing is wrong. Flippantly they explain, "On Fat Tuesday we live it up and on Ash Wednesday we give it up." So for the 40 days of lent before Easter, attempts are made to give up their ungodly ways.

For Christians who also face the temptation of sin, efforts must be made regularly to take off ungodliness. Anger must be controlled. Lying must stop. Bitterness must end. Retribution must be left to God. Bad language must be silenced. Ungodly behavior should no longer characterize the new creation.

Put on Godliness

The process of sanctification begins with death to sin and continues with daily dismissal of ungodly behaviors. The final step discussed by Paul in this process of sanctification is putting on godliness. Holy habits cannot be practiced until sinful behaviors are no longer present. Holy habits cannot be worn until unholy habits are removed. The Scripture gives positive instruction in righteousness.

Read again Colossians 3:12–14 to identify a believer's spiritual wardrobe. Listed below are the eight virtues a believer is to wear in order to be holy. Describe what each one means to you.

1. Heartfelt compassion ____________________________

2. Kindness ____________________________

3. Humility ____________________________

4. Gentleness ____________________________

5. Patience ____________________________

6. Tolerance ____________________________

7. Forgiveness ____________________________

8. Love ____________________________

Every believer is to put on "heartfelt compassion" or "tender mercy." The Hebrew word chesed, which is translated "mercy," literally means unfailing love. Do you wear tender mercy daily? "Kindness" has been defined as "steadfast love expressed in action." Do you express love consistently in your actions? "Humility" or total dependence on God and respect for others, not yourself, is to be worn by the believer. Does humility characterize your countenance? *Gentleness* or *meekness* is best described as "strength under control." Is your strength always under the control of God?

The Greek word for "longsuffering" or "patience" actually means "bear up under." Are you able to bear up under the challenges of your life? The believer is to put on "tolerance" or endurance of people, things, and circumstances. Can you tolerate even the most difficult people and the most challenging circumstances? The "forgiveness" expressed by a believer is from God and should be complete, everlasting, and readily available. Do you forgive others freely and without conditions?

Paul concludes his list of virtues with love—saving the best for last. Love is the most important garment in the spiritual wardrobe. True love, biblical love, is the finishing touch that makes the believer's ensemble complete or perfect. Do you put on love every day?

How do you feel when you add a finishing touch to your ensemble? Maybe you put on the perfect accessory, or carry a great-looking purse, or wear some shiny new shoes. You feel polished as your wardrobe comes together. A Christian should feel well dressed as each virtuous garment of the spiritual wardrobe is put on. (You can learn more about the spiritual wardrobe from the study of *A Woman's Guide to Spiritual Wellness,* the first book in this Bible study series.) Daily discipline is required to continue putting on godliness. Abiding in Christ enables you to put on and wear your spiritual wardrobe.

As you consider your spiritual wardrobe, determine ways you can put on godliness. List two or three specific ways for each virtue that you can practice godliness. As you write them down, make a commitment to begin living a life of holiness.

Heartfelt Compassion

1. ______________ 2. ______________ 3. ______________

Kindness

1. ______________ 2. ______________ 3. ______________

Humility

1. ______________ 2. ______________ 3. ______________

Gentleness

1. ______________ 2. ______________ 3. ______________

Patience

1. ______________ 2. ______________ 3. ______________

Tolerance

1. ______________ 2. ______________ 3. ______________

Forgiveness

1. ______________ 2. ______________ 3. ______________

Love

1. ______________ 2. ______________ 3. ______________

The psalmist gave instruction about developing holiness in Psalm 119:9–11. A believer is to keep her ways pure by obeying His Word, seeking His will, and abiding in His love. As the believer focuses on the positive traits to develop, she will not be discouraged by the negative behaviors to avoid. My dad often reminded me as I was growing up that if I would "spend all my time living for the Lord, I wouldn't have time to die for the devil." A life of holiness yields great joy. The Christian life is not a commitment to a boring life.

As you conclude this study, make a commitment to God to pursue this process of sanctification. You will need to renew this commitment regularly. Discipline yourself daily to develop holiness as you put sin to death, take off ungodliness, and put on godliness. You will discover that the development of holiness takes time. As Erwin W. Lutzer said, "There are no shortcuts to maturity. It takes time to be holy." But it is an investment of time that will bring forth great dividends in your personal life. Sing the words to this chorus as a closing response.

Take Time to Be Holy

Take time to be holy
Speak oft with the Lord
Abide in Him always
And feed on His Word
Make friends of God's children
Help those who are weak.
Forgetting in nothing
His blessings to seek.

Holy Scripture for Holy Living

Write the Scripture verse at the beginning of the chapter here. Then try to memorize it this week.

____

____

____

____

____

____

____

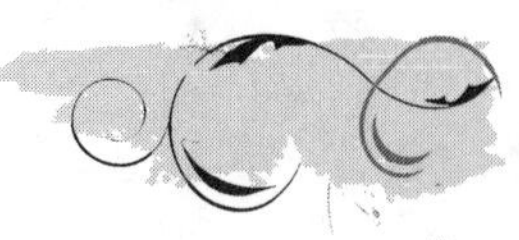

Practice Personal Holiness

List below those personal behaviors that God has convicted you to put to death, take off, and put on.

Put to Death _______________________________________

Take Off _______________________________________

Put On _______________________________________

Now pray that God will develop in you His holiness.

Lesson 6
An Unholy World

1 John 2:15—*"Do not love the world or the things that belong to the world."*

You don't have to look far to be reminded that we are living in an unholy world. Newspapers, magazines, television, and radio document the low level of human behavior today. In just a matter of days, the newspapers published the following headlines confirming an epidemic of unholiness.

"Five Shot, Four Stabbed in One Day"
"Congressman Accepts Money for Bribe"
"Defendant Guilty in Robbery of Tourist"
"Former Quarterback Shot Dead in Home"
"Serial Killings Spin Web of Fear"
"Marshals Siege Financier's Penthouse"
"Adulterous Governor Scorned by Wife"

While the Bible challenges Christians to be in the world but not of the world (Romans 12:1–2), holy rather than unholy, the reality is that the world bombards us with its unholiness. Sin is rampant and ungodliness is raging. A believer's greatest life work is resisting personal temptation and overcoming evil with good. But evil and wickedness are a natural part of human nature. They are intensifying in the world and confronting the Christian in the church.

The editor of a tabloid newspaper was brainstorming with his writers about a sensational headline. For a moment, they were stumped. It seemed that there had been no scandal, gossip, or personal calamity to report. With confidence, the editor assured his staff that a shocking headline would come—it always did. Sadly, he spoke from years of experience when he said, "You can always count on human nature for a scandal."

Sexual promiscuity is typical among young people today. Living together, hooking up, and one-night stands are not only accepted but expected. Even Christian youth wearing purity rings find themselves pregnant out of wedlock. Though biblical teachings about holy living are familiar, the unholy world has trapped believers in sin and unrighteousness.

Since sin entered the world, our lives have been unholy—filled with scandal. And the unholy world continues to influence Christians who have difficulty resisting sinful temptation. While there is little need to study about unholiness because it is so evident, Christians should turn to the Bible for guidance. Scripture, like the newspapers, records the sinful living of pagans and rebellious behavior of believers. Instead of focusing on unholiness though, let's examine what the Bible teaches about temptation, testing, and triumph over sin.

Temptation

Sin came into the world in the Garden of Eden. When Satan tempted Eve and Eve tempted Adam, the pattern was established (Genesis 3:1–19). No longer perfect and sinless, man and woman will inevitably face temptation and commit sin. Every person is tempted by someone or something. The world is filled with temptations, which makes sin an ever-present enemy of the believer. With the introduction of the Internet, temptation to sin is even greater in the privacy of a person's own home.

The reality of temptation is even greater today because of technology. Internet pornography has reached epidemic proportions because of accessibility. No longer must someone go to a store to buy a pornographic magazine. Turning on a computer without a filter can bring graphic pictures to the computer screen. Prime-time television now broadcasts programs once limited to X-rated movie theatres. Sexting explicit photos by telephone text messages spreads private images to the world. Temptation to view provocative pictures on the computer or watch risqué programs on the television is a daily reality for believers and unbelievers alike.

What does the Bible teach about temptation? Read 1 John 2:15–17. Then answer the following questions.

How does this Scripture describe temptation? ________________

____

Who is the tempter? ________________________________

What is the result of temptation? ________________________

God's Word clearly teaches that temptation is a part of life. It is *of* the world and *from* the world, not from God our Father. Temptation and its damaging consequences may last for a lifetime, but the will of God for holiness remains forever. What a profound biblical truth to help us combat temptation!

The Woman's Study Bible defines *temptation* as "an enticement to sin that arises from human desires and passions." Temptation comes in a variety of shapes and forms—thoughts, feelings, and actions. The tempter is the devil who is cunning and deceitful (Matthew 4:3). He quickly identifies human weakness and personalizes temptation in order to ensure the person's fall. Temptation was first recorded in the Book of Genesis and persisted throughout Scripture. Satan was so bold to tempt even Jesus Christ, the Son of God (Matthew 4:1–11). But Jesus proved that the power of God can triumph over temptation. When sin entered the world through Eve, Satan tempted, but Eve tasted.

The apostle John wrote and taught a lot about temptation. He warned the disciples and Christians in the early church about the temptations of the world and the flesh.

Underline the key words or phrases in the passages below where John warned about sin and worldliness.

John 15:19: *"If you were of the world, the world would love [you as] its own. However, because you are not of the world, but I have chosen you out of it, the world hates you."*

John 16:33: *"You will have suffering in this world. Be courageous! I have conquered the world."*

John 17:15: *"I am not praying that You take them out of the world, but that You protect them from the evil one."*

1 John 2:15: *"Do not love the world or the things that belong to the world. If anyone loves the world, love for the Father is not in him."*

1 John 3:6: *"Everyone who remains in Him does not sin; everyone who sins has not seen Him or known Him."*

Christians are to resist the temptation of the world—to avoid sinful influences whenever possible and to depend on the power of God to overcome the evil one. But the world is unholy and the devil is at work. God gives His children protection against warfare.

Read Ephesians 6:10–17 out loud. Claim this Scripture as your own as you resist temptation.

Testing

This unholy world is filled with temptation and testing. While temptation is the enticement to sin, testing involves obstacles that challenge the believer's personal relationship with the Lord. Testing begins at the time of conversion and continues until the believer is in the presence of God in heaven. Trials and tests of the faith can strengthen the believer (James 1:2–4). Tests come in a variety of forms: tests of knowing Him, tests of living for Him, and tests of serving Him.

John wrote very personally about the test of knowing God in 1 John 2:3–11. Read this passage in several translations. Then paraphrase it briefly in the space below.

____

____

____

____

One way that the devil tests believers is to prompt them to question their own salvation. Doubt, worry, and fear may cloud the mind of an uncertain Christian. Believers must cling tightly to the truth that salvation is secure. Once a person trusts the Lord as Savior, salvation is sure. The evil one and this unholy world will cast doubt and point blame if a believer does not show by her life that she is Christ's follower. The Apostle John confirmed the permanency of salvation and the evidence of salvation. *"This is how we are sure we have come to know Him: by keeping His commands"* (1 John 2:3).

Believers also experience the test of living for Him. It is so much easier to live life on your own terms and live like the world. But Christ calls Christians to a higher calling—holy living. Consistency in godly living will be tested. The devil will place obstacles to righteousness in the believer's path. He will challenge decisions and confuse thoughts in an attempt to seduce believers to his evil way. In 1 John 2, the apostle states clearly that the believer is to *"know Him"* (v. 3), *"love Him"* (v. 5), *"remain in Him"* (v. 6), and *"walk in Him"* (v. 6). You must live for the Lord and not just trust in Him as Savior.

Write your name in the blanks that follow and then read this personalized Scripture aloud as a prayer.

***If _______________ says she abides in Him then _______________ ought to walk just as He walked* (1 John 2:6).**

Put this verse with your name on a card and place it where you will notice it often and be reminded of your commitment to holiness.

Tests of faith face the believer who is trying to serve the Lord. While serving the Lord ought to be a blessing for the believer, ministry can often become difficult and burdensome. The devil will not only test our call to Christian service, but he will also question our motives and diminish the results. Tests of service confront even the most devoted, active servant of the Lord.

My husband, Chuck, and I faced a huge test of faith when our city and our seminary campus were devastated by Hurricane Katrina in August 2005. Our human natures questioned why so many selfless servants of the Lord lost all they had while many selfish sinners seemed untouched by disaster. Our campus experienced $75 million damage while the French Quarter had minimal loss. Questions filled our minds about our location in an area prone to storms and our ministry in a city facing such long-term recovery. As our faith was renewed and our confidence in the Lord was restored, we resumed serving the Lord confidently. In our greatest life trial, we experienced God's miraculous glory!

First John 2:5–6 is a promise for believers who are being tested. As you abide in Him and walk in His ways, you will grow in knowledge of Him. You will faithfully live for Him and sacrificially serve Him. What a great promise to claim as we respond to the testing of our faith!

Triumph

Though temptation and testing are inevitable in this unholy world, the believer must be reminded that God can triumph over the devil and his distractions. The believer must always be on the alert and consistently attest to faith in God demonstrated through words and actions. The power of God is available to believers who want to conquer sin. As the Scripture proclaims, *"The One who is in you is greater than the one who is in the world"* (1 John 4:4).

The Christians of the early church in Rome lived in an unholy world. They faced sinful temptation and spiritual testing. Paul wrote to encourage them to cling to their faith, remembering the high cost of sin. He used a familiar analogy from the slave market to help them understand the seriousness of their commitment to God. In Romans 6:15–23, Paul declared we are all slaves, either to sin or to God. When sin controls your life, you are a slave to unrighteousness. When God controls your life, you are a slave to righteousness. God can set you free from sin and give you the fruit of holiness. What a victory over death and sin!

For many years now, the New Orleans Baptist Theological Seminary has had a training program in Angola State Penitentiary. Louisiana's maximum security prison is filled with 5,000 men paying the price for their sins. Most of the prisoners are murderers, and most will never leave prison alive. But, many have turned to Jesus and been forgiven of their sins. They have been given a second chance and are now serving the Lord in their sentences. After graduating from the seminary, the prisoners are transferred to different cellblocks where churches are formed. Prisoner ministers lead lost to salvation and disciple others in the faith. Each graduation is a celebration of God's transforming love and a triumph over human transgression! A holy God brings about victorious life change in the unholiest of places.

Read the following Scriptures and note what they teach about triumph over temptation and testing.

Romans 8:2 ______________________________

John 8:34–36 ______________________________

John 8:31–32 ______________________________

Romans 5:9 ______________________________

Galatians 5:13–14 ______________________________

Romans 6:23 ______________________________

How reassuring are these Scriptures! Christ Jesus is the One who sets a believer free from sin (Romans 8:2). We no longer have to be slaves to sin (John 8:34–36). His truth can set us free (John 8:31–32). We are free from the judgment of God (Romans 5:9) and are free to serve Him and others (Galatians 5:13–14). Through Christ we can triumph over sin and death (Romans 6:23).

It is easy to feel oppressed in this unholy world, but there is *freedom* when you are a slave to God. It is natural to face temptation from the people and things of this world, but God can help you resist sin. It is common to question God and His work in the world, but He reassures you in these tests of faith. He can and will triumph over temptation and testing in your life.

How are you being tempted and tested? What entices you to sin? What challenges your faith? Circle the phrases on the next page that describe your own sinful nature.

1. Envious feelings

2. Sinful thoughts

3. Ungodly actions

4. Unkind words

5. Selfish passions

6. Other ______________________________

Has God helped you triumph over those ungodly thoughts and actions? Remember that He overwhelmingly conquers as you depend on Him to resist temptation.

As G. Campbell Morgan once said, "Holiness is not freedom from temptation, but power to overcome temptation." Make a personal commitment to resist temptation. Allow the Holy Spirit to make you a holy person in an unholy world. Experience the power of the Holy Spirit to overcome temptation and develop holiness.

Holy Scripture for Holy Living

Write the Scripture verse at the beginning of the chapter here. Then try to memorize it this week.

____

____

____

____

____

____

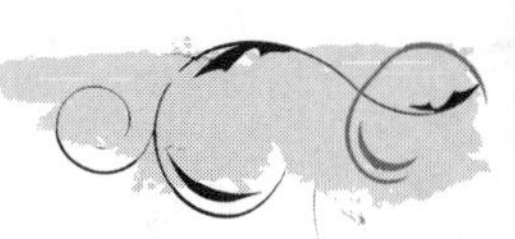

Practice Personal Holiness

Select a statement of truth below that you can commit to memorize and recall every time you face temptation in this unholy world.

> **"I will be holy in this unholy world."**
>
> **"God desires me to be holy, for He is holy."**
>
> **"I will be holy in all my conduct."**
>
> **"I will resist those temptations that lead to unholiness."**
>
> **"God can help me overcome even my greatest temptation."**
>
> **"With God's help I will triumph over temptation."**

Circle the statement that you selected. Now read it aloud prayerfully. God will bring it to your mind as you encounter temptation.

Lesson 7
Daily Holiness

Luke 9:23—*"If anyone wants to come with Me, he must deny himself, take up his cross daily, and follow Me."*

By this time in our study you may be convicted about your lack of holiness and your tendency to sin. Don't be discouraged! All of us are sinful by nature. Once God convicts you of your sinfulness, He begins to work in your heart and life to make you more like Him. Remember, *"If we confess our sins, He is faithful and righteous to forgive us our sins and to cleanse us from all unrighteousness"* (1 John 1:9). God can help you develop holy habits and live a holy lifestyle.

Becoming holy like God is a process. It is not just a one-step, short-term action. It is an ongoing, daily process. The believer must make a daily commitment to live a godly life if she is to resist temptation and be holy. The commitment must be sincere, serious, and specific. You must mean it before you can do it!

Before we go any further in this study, you must answer this very direct question:

Have you made a genuine commitment to holy living? Write your honest answer here.

____

____

____

____

If you answered yes, add to that commitment a promise to renew your personal commitment to the Lord *daily*. If you do not recommit yourself daily to a life of holiness, the world will have a stronger influence on you. If you do not make it a wholehearted commitment, the devil will discover your weaknesses and will not allow you to develop holiness.

In his suspense novel entitled *Compelling Evidence,* Steve Martini said, "The trouble most people have with resisting temptation is that they never really want to discourage it completely." This seems so true in our world and the Christian community. Even believers want to walk the line, live on both terms, and dabble with sin. Do you want to discourage temptation in your life? Do you sincerely want to be holy? If not, God will continue to convict you and correct you. If so, you must practice daily, the dedicated disciplines of holiness. Let's examine each step toward holiness.

Daily

Daily literally means every single day—without exception. It is 24/7—24 hours a day, 7 days a week—without holidays. What things do you do daily? Each of us performs important tasks daily. These are some things you do daily: breathe, brush your teeth, eat, dress, and bathe. You do them daily because they are necessary for your health and well-being. The Bible teaches that Christians must practice godliness daily if you desire to grow and thrive in your faith. Daily holiness is necessary for your spiritual health and vitality.

Look up a few Scriptures that instruct Christians on what to do and how to live daily. Beside each reference, record a life lesson to be practiced every day.

Psalm 61:8 ____________________

Psalm 72:15 ____________________

Psalm 88:9 ____________________

Isaiah 58:2 ____________________

Luke 9:23 ____________________

Acts 2:46–47 ______________________________

Acts 17:11 ______________________________

Hebrews 3:13 ______________________________

Scripture teaches that believers must behave in a certain way daily. In the Old Testament, we are taught to uphold our vow or commitment to God daily (Psalm 61:8). We should praise the Lord and call upon Him daily (Psalm 72:15; 88:9). Prayer and praise are daily habits of the holy. We should seek Him and His will daily (Isaiah 58:2).

The New Testament teaches us to worship Him daily, remaining constantly in His presence (Mark 14:49). We should take up the Cross every day, dying to self and following Him (Luke 9:23). Christians in the early church demonstrated that we should gather together daily for fellowship and worship (Acts 2:46–47). We should study the Scripture daily to know the truth (Acts 17:11). And we should encourage and minister to each other daily (Hebrews 3:13; 10:11). The days of a holy one will be very full! But these aren't things that will simply keep you busy. These daily disciplines determine the character and the lifestyle of the believer.

On a visit to an ancient Benedictine monastery in England, I was amazed by the schedule posted for the monks to follow. Waking at 3:00 A.M. for prayer and Scripture reading and working with their hands throughout the day seemed grueling. But, I was most startled to see that this same schedule applied to their lives every day of the year without exception. While Christians today do not lead that cloistered life of complete devotion, we must commit ourselves *daily* to a life of holiness. We must live for the Lord and *like* the Lord not just on Sundays but every day of the week.

How do you live every day? Is your daily life like your church life? Do you act, feel, and speak in a godly way on a daily basis? Is your life consistently holy? God desires His children to be holy like Him. His holiness is eternal. Our holiness should be a daily evidence of our commitment to Him.

Dedicated

In order to be consistent in our holy living, the believer must be dedicated—dedicated to the Lord and dedicated to living for Him daily. While our families and our work require dedication and commitment, our devotion to the Lord deserves our greatest dedication.

Do you know someone who is dedicated—truly devoted? List that person's name here and describe some behaviors that would document her dedication.

____

____

____

____

My precious mother-in-law is totally dedicated. She is completely sold out to Jesus and gives her whole self to Him. She is unwavering in her devotion to her husband and children. Also, she is a wholehearted, dedicated sports fan. When her Houston Astros baseball team struggles in the national playoffs, she has faith that they will win. Even when her Baylor Bears football team trails many points behind, she never gives up. Now, she is probably the most loyal fan of the New Orleans Saints. She always believes they can win. Christians are to *never give up* in our pursuit of holiness. God calls us to be dedicated to holy living. Daily holiness results from true dedication to the Lord.

Hannah dedicated her long-awaited son, Samuel, to the Lord. As a devoted follower of God, she desperately wanted her son to serve Him.

Read her heartwarming story in 1 Samuel 1:1 to 2:21.

Hannah obediently gave her child to God—the ultimate sacrifice for a loving mother. Leaving her child in the temple to serve the Lord, Hannah prayed to the holy God on behalf of her child. Her heart's desire was to be faithful and raise a son who was faithful. Hannah's sacrificial devotion was a testimony to young Samuel and has been an example for Christian mothers through the years. Samuel himself lived a holy life—a judge and prophet in Israel whose spiritual leadership turned that nation back to God. Hannah's dedication to holiness brought blessings to herself and her offspring. Her devotion to God has blessed believers throughout generations. Are you willing to be dedicated like Hannah—giving up what you love most to be obedient to God, to be holy like Him?

Disciplined

A believer must practice spiritual disciplines in order to live a holy life. Holiness does not come naturally. It is not easy. It takes effort and persistence. Discipline in holiness is necessary every day. *Discipline* is "training that corrects, molds, or perfects the mental faculties, or moral character." Holiness requires control and effort—it doesn't just happen. Training and tenacity are needed.

Christians have the power of God as an added source to their own self-control. I call that "divine discipline," Spirit-controlled discipline of oneself, God's power plus my power. If God convicts you of a need for more personal discipline, you may benefit from reading my testimony in *Divine Discipline: How to Develop and Maintain Self-Control*. Personal and spiritual discipline is necessary for the believer to live a holy life. Let's consider the spiritual disciplines that are essential to holiness.

What are some spiritual disciplines that you believe a Christian should practice in order to be holy? List several specific disciplines below.

______________________ ______________________

______________________ ______________________

______________________ ______________________

Daily discipline is essential to spiritual growth and maturity in the believer's life. Increased knowledge of God and persistence in obeying God should result in holiness. If that is true, spiritual discipline and holy living are dependent upon each other. Let's take time to discuss several spiritual disciplines: Bible study, prayer, fellowship, service, witnessing, and meditation. While this is not an exhaustive list of spiritual disciplines, these spiritual disciplines are necessary for daily holiness.

1. Bible Study

Most Christians believe the Bible is God's Holy Word and trust it as truth, but so few actually study it. Personal, in-depth Bible study is essential for spiritual growth and daily holiness. The Bible teaches us about God and His statutes, makes us aware of sin, and helps us live godly lives (Psalm 119:9–11; Hebrews 5:12–14). Do you spend time daily studying the Bible? Are you disciplined in the study of His Word? Do you know more about the Bible today than when you came to faith in Him? It's not too late to begin or resume your daily Bible study.

Make a plan for personal Bible study and stick with it so you can develop daily holiness. Record below your specific commitments to study God's Word.

____

____

____

____

2. Prayer

Spiritual discipline includes daily prayer, as well as regular Bible study. Prayer is communication with God. Conversation with the Father not only strengthens your relationship with Him, a spirit of prayer also promotes holiness. In order to keep prayer a priority in your life, set a time and place for prayer. Select some prayer resources such as books on prayer and keep a prayer list or prayer journal. How long has it been since you prayed? How long did you pray? And are you continuing in a spirit of prayer throughout your day?

Set some goals to develop the daily discipline of prayer.

____

____

____

3. Fellowship

Biblical fellowship is the bonding together or joining together of those devoted to God. Fellowship or communion with God through prayer and Bible study builds your relationship with Him. The more fellowship, the tighter the bond. We are also to have fellowship with God's church and His children. Regular participation in worship and attendance in church strengthen the relationship with God too. It is not always easy or enjoyable to attend church, but corporate worship strengthens your faith. Believers also benefit from fellowship with other believers. Fellowship promotes daily holiness. My husband says, "Christians are like bananas—they grow best in bundles." So be actively involved in fellowship with other believers.

Identify several specific disciplines to strengthen your fellowship in each of these areas so you can be disciplined in holiness.

God—______________________________

His Church—__________________________

His Children—_________________________

4. Service

A disciplined believer will be involved in serving others. The servant spirit of Jesus was reflected in His unending ministry to others. Believers who are growing in the Lord daily should desire to serve others willingly and unselfishly. But ministry takes time and effort. It is worth it though because of earthly blessings and eternal rewards. Ministry begins with your family and continues with your neighbors and even strangers. Are you involved in ministry to others? How do you serve others? Discipline yourself to serve faithfully as Jesus did every day.

Recall five acts of service you rendered to others this week. Ask God to help you develop your servanthood.

1. ______________________________

2. ______________________________

3. ______________________________

4. ______________________________

5. ______________________________

5. Witnessing

One of the toughest spiritual disciplines is witnessing or evangelism. While most Christians believe evangelism should be a priority for the church, few actually witness. Few Christians make witnessing a priority in their own lives. Christians must discipline themselves daily to be witnesses. Discipline is necessary for believers to talk about their faith. My husband, Chuck, who is an evangelism professor, says, "Witnessing should be the natural result of a heart warmed in the presence of God, a life that resembles the life of Jesus, and a genuine concern for other people." Is your heart on fire for God? Is your life a testimony of Him? Are you burdened for lost people you know? Discipline your heart and your life and you can become a daily witness.

Fill in specific names in this sentence of commitment as you discipline yourself to be a witness. I will speak a word of witness this week to ______________, ______________, and ______________. Pray for the lost people you know and be determined to share a witness with them.

6. Meditation
Even the world today recognizes the benefit of meditation. World religions and yoga enthusiasts recommend regular periods of meditation for their followers to reduce stress and get in tune with their spirits. God was the first person to recommend meditation to His followers. Meditation for the believer is focusing thoughts on God, listening to Him, thinking about His teachings, being still in His presence. Joshua 1:8 says, "This book of instruction must not depart from your mouth, you are to recite it day and night, so that you may carefully observe everything written in it. For then you will prosper and succeed in whatever you do." Strength and power come to the believer in times of meditation. Holy living is a natural result of daily meditation on God and His Word. The psalmist gave instruction about meditation: *"His delight is in the LORD's instruction, and he meditates on it day and night" (Psalm 1:2)*.

Pause right now for five minutes to focus on the Lord. Think of Him, His glory and His goodness. Don't let your thoughts wander to other things. Commit to meditating on the Lord every day.

In his well-known book, *Celebration of Discipline,* Richard Foster honestly acknowledges the challenge of the disciplined life and thoroughly discusses specific spiritual disciplines. He affirms the necessity of discipline for Christian living and suggests various ways to pursue discipline. But, Foster's most encouraging promise is the reward of discipline—freedom. He summarizes, "the purpose of the Disciplines is liberation from the stifling slavery to self-interest and fear" (p. 2). What a hope and confidence in the Lord!

The life of holiness does not simply come from desire. Holy living results only when the believer makes a *daily* commitment to be *dedicated* to the Lord and *disciplined* in godliness. What a challenge! Athletes face this challenge as they train for the Olympics. They must practice their sport daily, be dedicated wholeheartedly, and be disciplined in training. Then they can compete and may even win. Believers face this challenge as we run this race called life. We must live for the Lord daily; be dedicated wholeheartedly to Him; and be disciplined in spiritual matters. Then we can successfully compete and will win an eternal reward.

Holy Scripture for Holy Living

Write the Scripture verse at the beginning of the chapter here. Then try to memorize it this week.

____

____

____

____

You will not be able to succeed in daily holiness without dedication and discipline.

Practice Personal Holiness

List below a specific goal in each spiritual discipline. Then commit these plans to the Lord.

1. Bible study ________________________________

2. Prayer ________________________________

3. Fellowship ________________________________

4. Service ________________________________

5. Witnessing ________________________________

6. Meditation ________________________________

You will achieve daily holiness as you practice these spiritual disciplines daily!

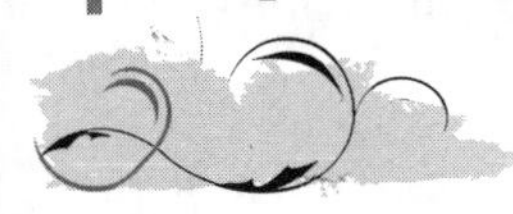

Lesson 8
Holy Habits

Ephesians 4:24 — *"You put on the new man, the one created according to God's [likeness] in righteousness and purity of the truth."*

Habits are behaviors that shape a character. They can strengthen or weaken a person. Good habits help a person while bad habits hurt. That is why there has been extensive teaching about habits throughout history. At the turn of the twentieth century, Samuel Smiles said:

Sow a thought and you reap an act;
Sow an act and you reap a habit;
Sow a habit and you reap a character;
Sow a character and you reap a destiny.

Now at the turn of the twenty-first century, we can echo his truths. Many bad thoughts lead to unholy habits. And those unholy habits result in a very ungodly world. It is encouraging to realize that good thoughts can lead to holy habits, and holy habits can shape our character and change the world.

What is a habit? Write your personal definition here.

____

____

____

____

____

Many people identify a habit as bad manners or irritating behavior like cracking your knuckles or chewing with your mouth open. Others think a habit is something you do unconsciously, without thinking, like biting your fingernails or smacking your lips. But a habit is actually a much broader behavior, a more general action. A habit is defined as a manner of conducting oneself or a settled tendency or usual manner of behavior. More specifically, a habit is a behavior pattern acquired by frequent repetition that has become nearly or completely involuntary.

With those definitions in mind, what are some of your own personal habits?

____

____

____

____

____

____

____

____

Are those habits good or bad, holy or unholy?

In his book, *The Pursuit of Holiness,* Jerry Bridges identifies four principles about holiness. These practical lessons will help us understand why believers must develop holy habits. The first principle is that "habits are developed and reinforced by frequent repetition." Anything that is done over and over will become a habit. Saying no to sin over and over again results in holy habits. The second principle is "never let an exception occur." If you allow an exception for sin, you reinforce the old habits of ungodliness. The third principle is that "diligence in all areas is required to ensure success in one area." A believer must energetically pursue holiness in all aspects of life so that she will be holy in at least one. And the last principle is "don't be discouraged by failure." Sinful nature causes failures in holy living, but God forgives and restores a believer who keeps on trying to live a holy life and develop holy habits. These principles of holiness are encouraging and inspiring.

Old Habits—New Habits

Paul wrote about the habits of the old man and new man in his letter to the Christians in Ephesus. Many of the less mature believers had failed to develop new godly habits of behavior. Though converted, they were continuing their old sinful habits. Paul confronted them directly, criticizing their ungodly behavior and characterizing their desired godly lifestyles.

Read Ephesians 4:17–32. Then write a descriptive contrast between the old man in sin and the new man in Christ.

Old Man	New Man
______________________	______________________
______________________	______________________
______________________	______________________
______________________	______________________
______________________	______________________
______________________	______________________
______________________	______________________
______________________	______________________

Believers are no longer to live the sinful lifestyle of the old life. Instead the believer is to develop new thought patterns and behaviors—holy habits. Intimacy with God should replace alienation from God. Wisdom should replace ignorance. Clear knowledge of God's will should replace blindness by sin.

There is a growing trend among some young ministers to become more appealing to the world. They condone drinking and use profanity supposedly in an effort to relate. Their churches host wine and cheese parties, and they show pornographic movies all in an attempt to reach the lost world. How sad! What a clear violation of Scripture that teaches believers to develop a new nature and holy habits. Much work must be done to reach the world and the church. Godliness is necessary to make a difference in their lives.

The Christians in Ephesus had become lewd, unclean, and greedy. God, through Jesus Christ, forgave their sin and made each of them a new creation—a *holy* being, not just a human being. As a result, they stopped lying, stealing, nagging, and blaming. They started loving, encouraging, and forgiving. Those Christians developed some holy habits. God can do the same work of transformation today. We need to follow in obedience, repeating those thoughts and actions that can become holy habits—evidence of the new creation in Christ.

Read the following Scriptures and fill in the blanks to list some of the holy habits that believers should develop through frequent repetition.

1. ***"You must not ____________. You must not act ____________ or ____________________ to one another'"* (Leviticus 19:11).**

2. **"__________ *the Lord your God and follow His* ____________" (Deuteronomy 27:10).**

3. ***"Serve the LORD with ___________."* Praise and pray without ceasing (Psalm 2:11).**

4. _______________ Scripture and meditate on the Word, applying it to your life (Psalm 119:11).

5. *"The entirety of Your word is _______________, and all Your righteous judgements endure forever"* (Psalm 119:160).

6. *"_____________ hands make one poor, but ___________ hands bring riches"* (Proverbs 10:4).

7. *"Love your _____________ and _____________ for those who persecute you"* (Matthew 5:44).

8. Practice the golden rule. *"Do unto ____________ as you would have them do unto ________________"* (Matthew 7:12 KJV).

9. Observe all God's ____________. God is _____________ with you (Matthew 28:20).

10. Be devoted to _____________, _____________, _____________, and ____________________ with other believers (Acts 2:42).

11. *"Flee from ___________ ___________! Every sin a person can commit is...against his own"* ___________ (1 Corinthians 6:18).

12. *"Love is _____________; love is ___________. Love does not ___________; is not ___________; is not ___________"* (1 Corinthians 13:4).

13. *"Love your ________________ as ________________"* (Galatians 5:14).

14. Use ______________ language in all your conversation. Let your words build up and give grace (Ephesians 4:29).

15. ________________ others freely and unconditionally as God so freely ________________ you (Ephesians 4:32).

16. Be ______________ where you go and what you do. You are always a witness (Ephesians 5:15).

17. Stand up for what you believe. Be __________________ in your faith (Ephesians 6:10).

18. *"Rejoice and share your ______________ with [others]"* (Philippians 2:17–18).

19. Think pure ____________. Put away sinful ideas (Philippians 4:8).

20. *"__________ in Him;...overflowing with __________"* (Colossians 2:6–7).

21. ___________ others in words and deeds. Put the needs of others before your own (1 Thessalonians 5:11).

22. Make ______________________ a constant part of your day (1 Thessalonians 5:17).

23. Be ______________________________, sharing all that you have with others (1 Timothy 6:18).

24. Don't be ____________ of the Lord. Share a word of ______ ________ (2 Timothy 1:8).

25. *"Do not ____________ about one another."* Be positive in your attitude and actions (James 5:9).

Samuel Johnson once said that the chains of habit are too weak to be felt until they are too strong to be broken. What a profound statement! Are you developing holy habits that are growing too strong to be broken? As your holy habits strengthen your faith, you will not only grow but also you will go on living for the Lord. You will remain holy in this unholy world!

Holy Scripture for Holy Living

Write the Scripture verse at the beginning of the chapter here. Then try to memorize it this week.

____

____

____

____

Practice Personal Holiness

Has God convicted you of some ungodly habits? Has He challenged you to develop some new godly habits? Be specific as you list them below.

Old Habits ______________________________________

____

____

New Habits ______________________________________

____

____

Claim God's promise in Ephesians 4:24 that He can create in you a new person of righteousness and purity of the truth.

Lesson 9
The Pursuit of Holiness

Hebrews 12:14 — *"Pursue peace with everyone, and holiness — without it no one will see the Lord."*

Holiness is not a status to be achieved, but a life goal to be pursued. Because we are human, no man or woman can ever be holy like God. Every believer, however, should pursue holiness. Pursuit requires effort and hard work. Pursuit implies a lifelong task. Pursuit demands discipline but results in difference — a different life.

Hebrews 12:14 says to *"pursue peace with everyone, and holiness — without it no one will see the Lord."* When believers have an active and growing relationship with God, their pursuit of holiness will be a vital part of living.

Read Hebrews 12:14 in several translations. Write the verse in your own words as you decide to pursue holiness.

____

____

____

____

____

Pursue, strive for, seek, work toward holiness. Our challenge as believers is to become more holy every day. Holiness will not just happen. It must be persistently pursued.

The prophet Isaiah proclaimed the holiness of God and challenged the children of God to be holy. In Isaiah 6, the holiness of God was announced in the temple and the holiness of God was to be lived out in His people. Isaiah gave a visual image that helps us understand how we must pursue holiness.

Read Isaiah 6:1–8. Underline the threefold holy and any other words that describe the holiness of God.

Can you picture the temple with the Lord sitting high up on His throne? While our Holy God reigns from His throne in heaven, He also reigns over the world and in our lives. Around the temple, there were seraphim (fiery creatures with six wings) guarding the holiness of God. As the seraphim positioned their wings, they instructed God's children in the pursuit of holiness.

Reread Isaiah 6:2. How were the wings of the seraphim positioned? Complete the following phrases:

with two wings they covered their ______________________

with two wings they covered their ______________________

with two wings they ________________________________

The placement of their wings symbolizes aspects of personal holiness. With two wings, the seraphim covered his face, indicating reverence. With two wings he covered his feet, depicting humility. And with two wings he flew, demonstrating service. The pursuit of holiness involves reverence, humility, and service. Let's examine each part of the pursuit.

Fear God

The seraphim's first indication of the pursuit of holiness was the covering of his eyes in reverence. Those fiery creatures expressed respect for God as they hid their eyes before an awesome God.

Look up the word *reverence* in the dictionary to understand better this response. Write your definition here.

___

___

___

Reverence is profound respect and love, awesome fear and dread. A believer's pursuit of holiness begins with total fear of God, not panic or dread but deep awe and respect. The Bible teaches that the fear of the Lord is the beginning of knowledge (Proverbs 1:7) and that the consequences of sin should be feared (Proverbs 28:1–4). What else does the Bible teach about the fear of the Lord?

Read the following verses and record a biblical teaching about the fear of God beside each reference.

Proverbs 2:5 ___

___

Proverbs 9:10 ___

___

Proverbs 14:26–27 ___

___

Proverbs 15:33 ___

___

Proverbs 22:4 ___

___

The fear of God leads to an understanding of Him and His holiness (Proverbs 2:5; 9:10). The fear of God gives confidence and life (Proverbs 14:26,27). The fear of the Lord gives instruction and leads to humility (Proverbs 15:33). And the fear of God results in blessings and honor (Proverbs 22:4). Believers should be inspired by the Word to fear God.

Do you fear God? Do you hold Him in your highest regards? Do you completely respect Him and look up to Him? In life you have probably looked up to people – people you admired and respected. Profound respect is often given to ministers who are the Lord's servants. As we look up to them, we are revering God. What a responsibility ministers have to live worthy of human respect.

Mary of Bethany demonstrated her fear of God when out of profound respect and deep love, she anointed the feet of Jesus with very costly oil (John 12:3). Read her precious story in John 12:1–8 to see a powerful demonstration of reverence.

How do you show respect to God? What are some specific ways you demonstrate your fear of God?

____

____

____

____

Do you relish God's presence? Do you bask in His love? Do you call out to Him in love? Do you seek His face? Do you honor His name? Those who truly respect God respect His person, His people, and His place. If you honestly desire to pursue holiness, you must fear God and commit yourself to Him. You must love Him with all your heart, and seek Him with all your soul. You must hold Him up and worship Him. Your profound love for Him will be reflected in your respect of His children and your love of His house. Those who fear God will pursue Him and pursue holiness.

Humble Yourself

The seraphim also depicted the importance of humility by covering their feet with two of their wings. While reverence is the first step in a believer's pursuit of holiness, humility is the natural next step. When a believer realizes who God is, she quickly realizes who she is not. Humility is a natural result of reverence.

The New Testament teaches that humility is total dependence on God and respect for others. Humility is not a weakness but a strength from God. Because human nature is selfish and proud, the pursuit of holiness demands unselfish humility. A believer must be humbled before a very holy God.

Humility is not a trait pursued by the world. In fact, the Greek world and our present world abhor the quality of humility. Humility is seen by the world as a sign of weakness and inferiority. Therefore, humility is a virtue that sets believers apart—makes us holy like Him.

Fill in the blanks below to indicate how God rewards the humble.

***He topples the mighty and ____________________ the lowly* (Luke 1:52).**

***"Humble yourselves before the Lord, and He will ____________ you"* (James 4:10).**

***"Humble yourselves therefore under the mighty hand of God, so that He may exalt you in ________________ time"* (1 Peter 5:6).**

The Lord criticizes the proud and exalts the humble (Luke 1:52). He lifts up or exalts those who bow their knees before Him (James 4:10). He exalts those who are humble in His own due time (1 Peter 5:6). While the world may not reward meekness and humility, God honors those believers who humble themselves in their pursuit of holiness.

Jesus who was God in the flesh, the all-powerful One, lived a humble life. He was born in a stable, raised by a carpenter, and wore no earthly crown. He served others and cared for the least of all people. In a complete act of humility, Jesus washed the feet of His disciples (John 13:1–11).

The Apostle Paul reflected on the humble spirit of a co-laborer named Phoebe. While little is known about this sweet sister in the faith, her humble spirit is recorded for all time. We are encouraged to imitate her humble spirit.

Read her brief story in Romans 16:1–2. Note Paul's accolades. How did he describe her?

____

____

____

____

____

Phoebe, who humbly served the Lord and His church, was called by Paul sister, servant, saint, helper. Her humble service demonstrated her holiness and resulted in her praise. While the world does not recognize the humble, the Lord does. A pursuit of holiness begins with attitudes of reverence and humility.

Serve Others

With two of their wings, the seraphim covered their faces in reverence and with two wings they covered their feet in humility. With the last two of their wings the seraphim flew. We must learn to serve others as we pursue holiness. However, service does not begin the pursuit of holiness. From a heart of love and humility, service will overflow. Service to others should be the natural result of a holy life.

Service in the Bible actually refers to joy in doing for others, in meeting their needs. Ministry and service put feet to a heart of holiness.

Circle each biblical teaching about service in the following Scriptures.

Matthew 20:28: *"The Son of Man did not come to be served, but to serve, and to give His life—a ransom for many."*

John 12:26: *"If anyone serves Me, he must follow Me. Where I am, there My servant also will be. If anyone serves Me, the Father will honor him."*

Romans 12:11: *"Do not lack diligence; be fervent in spirit; serve the Lord."*

Galatians 5:13: *"For you are called to freedom, brothers; only don't use this freedom as an opportunity for the flesh, but serve one another through love."*

Ephesians 6:6–7: *"As slaves of Christ, do God's will from your heart. Render service with a good attitude, as to the Lord and not to men."*

Are you involved in service? Is your commitment to holiness being expressed through ministry to others? If so, you are being obedient to God's will for His people. If not, you need to renew a commitment to the pursuit of holiness and service to others. Make service to the Lord and service to others major life priorities.

Since the devastation of Hurricane Katrina in 2005, thousands of volunteers have served the people of New Orleans and the Gulf South. Hours of hard labor have been extended by strangers to help rebuild homes, restore churches, and revitalize communities. Without the diligent labor of these tireless volunteers, little progress would have been made. For many, their service was a natural result of their love of God and a humble desire to help others in need.

Dorcas was a woman in the early church who reflected God's holiness in her life of service. The Scripture says, *"She was always doing good works and acts of charity"* (Acts 9:36). Dorcas not only noticed the needs of those around her but also did something to meet those needs. Using her ability to sew, Dorcas made clothes for the widows in her hometown. Her ministry to them was so significant that the women grieved deeply when she died. God, through the apostle Peter, gave life back to Dorcas so she could continue serving others. Her consistent holiness was a lifestyle witness and her dedicated service was a life-changing ministry. Let Dorcas be an example of service for you.

Are you pursuing holiness? Is a life of holiness a daily commitment for you? How do you show your love and respect for God? Have you humbled yourself in total dependence upon God? Are you joyfully serving others? God who is Holy desires His children to be holy—holy as well as happy. Oswald Chambers said it this way: "The destined end of man is not happiness nor health but holiness."

Holiness is not what God does but who God is. The pursuit of holiness for the believer should be the lifelong effort of becoming holy like God. Don't be focused on doing good, but becoming holy. Many believers get off track in their pursuit of holiness when they busy themselves *doing* and don't allow God to perfect His holiness in them.

Holy Scripture for Holy Living

Write the Scripture verse at the beginning of the chapter here. Then try to memorize it this week.

____

____

____

____

____

____

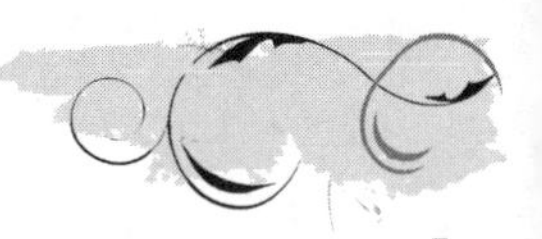

Practice Personal Holiness

Take a moment to do a personal evaluation of your life in Christ. Are you becoming holy like your Holy God? Are you pursuing holiness daily? Are you renewing your commitment to holy living every day? Do you feel you are making progress in your pursuit of holiness?

Give a specific example below of how your holiness is being reflected through reverence, humility, and service. How have you recently demonstrated your holiness? List some ways under these categories.

Fear of God ____________________________________

Humility of self ________________________________

Service to others _______________________________

Praise the Lord with the seraphim as you proclaim, *"Holy, holy, holy is the Lord of Hosts; His glory fills the whole earth"* (Isaiah 6:3).

Lesson 10
The Fruit of Holiness

Romans 6:22 — *"But now, since you have been liberated from sin, and become enslaved to God, you have your fruit, which results in sanctification — and the end is eternal life!"*

While we shouldn't be holy just to receive rewards, what a joy to know we do receive blessings for our holiness. Believers should ask the questions, *What is the evidence of holiness in our lives? What is the fruit of holiness?* In the answers to these questions are often the blessings of giving our holiness as an offering to the Lord while we live in an unholy world.

Scripture speaks a lot about fruit, not just the edible kind. *Fruit* is first introduced in Genesis when God created the grass and trees. He specified that the fruit tree yields fruit according to its own kind (Genesis 1:11). Fruit is the product of the specific tree. An apple tree produces apples. This basic biblical principle teaches that the kind of tree affects the product of the tree. Thus a holy life will produce holy fruit.

Later in Genesis it was the fruit eaten by Adam and Eve that brought sin into the world (Genesis 3:6). The fruit or harvest of the land was given as an offering to the Lord (Genesis 4:3). Children were called the fruit of the womb, a blessing from God (Genesis 30:2 KJV). The Psalms speak often of fruit as evidences of a godly life (Psalm 1:3; 92:14; 104:13). The Proverbs also refer to fruit as the works of God (Proverbs 8:19; 11:30). The prophets describe the fruit as the results of their doings (Isaiah 3:10; Jeremiah 6:19; Ezekiel 17:8–9; Daniel 4:20–22; Hosea 10:1, 13; Amos 6:12). The Old Testament is filled with these and many other references about fruit.

In the New Testament, *fruit* most often refers to the work of the Holy Spirit in a believer's life (Galatians 5:22–23). Fruit is a result of righteousness (Philippians 1:11; James 3:18) and a picture of new believers (Romans 1:13; 1 Corinthians 16:15). Fruit may sometimes communicate a sense of reward or blessing (John 4:36; Philippians 4:17).

Examine the Scriptures above. What do you understand the *word* fruit to mean in the Bible? Write your ideas here.

____

____

____

____

The fruit of the Holy Spirit is a wonderful study. If you haven't personally examined this biblical teaching, I encourage you to do so. You could simply study the primary passage in Galatians 5:22–25. Or you could complete a more in-depth study using materials available in your local Christian bookstore. But for the purposes of our study of personal holiness, let's focus on what the Bible says about the rewards of holiness.

Before we investigate other fruit of holiness, take a few moments to consider evidences of holiness in your own life. As you think of them, list how you have demonstrated the fruit of the Spirit mentioned in Galatians 5.

Fruit of the Spirit (Galatians 5:22–23)	Fruit of Holiness (My Life)
Love	______________________
Joy	______________________
Peace	______________________
Patience	______________________

Kindness ____________________

Goodness ____________________

Faithfulness ____________________

Gentleness ____________________

Self-control ____________________

In her Bible study *Living Beyond Yourself*, Beth Moore says that while the fruit of the Holy Spirit—love, joy, peace, patience, kindness, goodness, faithfulness, gentleness, and self-control—is living proof that the Spirit of God dwells in you, the Bible also teaches about other fruit of holiness. Now let's consider these and other blessings of the holy life.

Joy

A primary fruit of holiness is *joy*—not just happiness or pleasure. True joy is a profound sense of excitement that results from knowing and serving God. It is truly the fruit or blessing of a right relationship with God.

Those who live holy lives experience true joy. Joy also encourages holiness. Jerry Bridges, author of *The Pursuit of Holiness*, said, "Joy not only results from a holy life, but there is also a sense in which joy helps produce a holy life."

Do you believe that joy is a fruit of holiness? If so, write the word *joy* in the statement below.

God gives abundant ________________ to those who obediently follow Him and live holy lives.

Jesus Himself said that joy would be given to those who obey Him (John 15:10–11). Thus, only those who are pursuing holiness as a way of life will receive abundant joy from God the Father.

Think about joy—true joy. What kind of life produces true joy?

____

____

Would you receive greater joy from living a sinful life or a holy life?

____

____

Why? ____

____

____

For about 17 years, my dad lived a life separated from the Lord. During that time, he sought happiness in the world. Finally, in his despair, he returned to the Lord and found true joy in obedience. This evangelist, well known for his message "It's Fun Being Saved," learned personally that joy only comes in holy living. We who love my dad rejoice today to see his godly life.

God clearly calls His children to live holy lives, and He rewards the righteous for their goodness. Abundant blessings are experienced by those who live holy lives. Are you filled with the joy of the Lord? If not, you may not be walking in holiness. Sin can rob you of your joy (Psalm 51:8, 12). Joy will return when the believer walks in holiness.

Wisdom

Another fruit of holiness is wisdom. Wisdom is generally thought to be accumulated learning, discernment, or good sense. The Bible says wisdom is from God and that God is all-knowing (omniscient) or wise. As children of God make godly choices and live holy lives, God gives them wisdom to know Him and His will.

James 3:13–18 contrasts heavenly wisdom and demonic wisdom or wisdom from God and wisdom from the devil. Read this passage and list some differences between heavenly wisdom and earthly wisdom.

Heavenly Wisdom	**Earthly Wisdom**
______________________	______________________
______________________	______________________
______________________	______________________
______________________	______________________
______________________	______________________

While God gives heavenly wisdom to those who obey Him, the devil offers earthly wisdom to those who live by their own desires. James 3:13–18 clearly teaches that those who are truly wise show good conduct (v. 13) and sow the fruit of righteousness (v. 18). As believers make wise decisions, they develop holy lifestyles. And as believers live out God's holiness, they become wiser. Wisdom is evident when a believer leads a life marked by purity, peace, gentleness, a yielding spirit, good fruits without partiality and hypocrisy. In other words, a believer's holiness is a sign of wisdom.

I highly value education. After 25 straight years of school, I received my PhD and learned how much I still did not know. It is important for people to gain knowledge and grow mentally. However, for Christians, wisdom from the Lord is more desirable. Through Bible study and prayer, believers learn about God and His ways. In the process of sanctification, we should become more like Him—holy. Our holy lives are then reflections of wisdom we receive from the Lord.

Freedom

Let's discuss one more fruit of holiness—*freedom*. Freedom is the absence of bondage; it is total liberation. As a believer lives a holy life, there is great freedom. The believer is no longer enslaved to sin but free in Christ. Holiness does lead to freedom.

In the Book of Romans, Paul wrote about death to sin, and life in Christ. Then in chapter 6, the apostle used the analogy of slavery to help the Christian understand that a sinful life leads to bondage and a righteous life leads to freedom.

Read Romans 6:22 and write its meaning in your own words.

____

____

____

Salvation is delivery not only from the penalty of sin but also from the power of sin. When a believer professes faith in Jesus Christ, a holy life should result. The gift of God for salvation is eternal life—the fruit of salvation is holiness and the fruit of holiness is freedom. It is freedom from the penalty of sin and freedom to pursue holiness.

In his book *The Way of Holiness,* Stephen Olford talks about the different ways the fruit of holiness is evidenced in a believer's life. If you are truly living a holy life, you should bear fruit or yield a harvest in every area of your life, including your worship, your walk, and your work. How fruitful are you? Are you releasing the Spirit in your life? Have you grown closer to God in your daily life?

Rate your personal fruitfulness in each of these areas. On a scale from 1 to 5, with 1 being the lowest and 5 the highest, circle a number below that honestly reflects your fruitfulness in…

Your Christian Worship	1	2	3	4	5
Your Christian Walk	1	2	3	4	5
Your Christian Work	1	2	3	4	5

As you conclude this study on the fruit of holiness, reflect on the fruit you bear and rejoice in the fruitfulness of others.

When I was a senior in high school, I was totally surprised when my classmates elected me "Miss John F. Kennedy High School." I determined to live a godly life as one of the few Christians in my school. My behavior was so unlike the other students. So, I was clueless as to why they would honor me. When I shared my question with my mother, she wisely advised me that God was honoring my commitment to Him. He gave me a reward for holiness that I never expect. He continually blesses us for our holiness.

Holy Scripture for Holy Living

Write the Scripture verse at the beginning of the chapter here. Then try to memorize it this week.

____

____

____

____

____

____

____

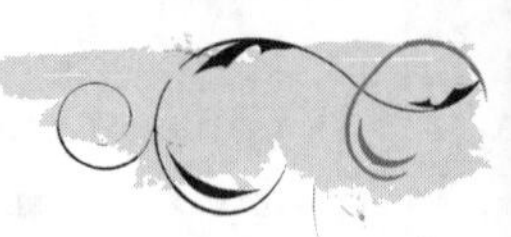

Practice Personal Holiness

List the fruit of holiness in your life. Thank God for the evidence of His work in your life!

____

____

____

Now pray for God to convict you of your need to bear more fruit of holiness.

What works of the Holy Spirit do you desire to develop in your life?

____

____

____

God wants you to bear the fruit of holiness. He can do it through you!

Lesson 11
The Influence of Holiness

Psalm 111:9—*"He has sent redemption to His people. He has ordained His covenant forever. His name is holy and awe-inspiring."*

In a very ungodly world, the believer often feels hopeless in the task of reaching the world for Christ. However, we must not be discouraged but be even more committed to live holy lives. We need to understand that even one godly person can have a powerful influence. After all, it took only one river to carve the Grand Canyon.

St. John Chrysostom said, "If but ten among us lead a holy life, we shall kindle a fire which shall light up the entire city." Because of the power of the Holy Spirit, even a few believers can have a profound influence in this ungodly world. Your holy life counts; it counts for eternity!

In a previous chapter, I mentioned our seminary's training program at Angola State Penitentiary. What a powerful real-life example of one changed life influencing the prison for good! The holy lives of our students shine in the darkness of that place. And, over time, those holy lives have made a difference. Hundreds of inmates have come to know the Lord as Savior because of the influence of a few godly men.

Influence is the power exerted over the minds or behavior of others. It can be a spiritual or moral force, a positive or negative power, or a godly or ungodly witness. People can truly have influence on other people. The greatest influence on a believer's life should be Jesus Christ—His perfect life and His power to save. Women of the Bible can also be a powerful influence on Christian women today. Many godly women throughout history have had great impact on others, and many women today who are dedicated to the Lord have a profound influence. Women have the real ability to influence others to God and holy living.

What woman has had a profound influence on your life?

____

Why? ____

____

How has her influence affected your life? _________________

____

God calls each of us to be an influence in our world, our church, our community, and our family. We cannot have a godly influence without living a holy life. Words alone do not make a godly impact; it takes a holy life. You have the power to determine whether your influence will be for good or for evil. Let's consider the power of holiness as you make a commitment to influence others to witness, to serve, and to love.

Power to Witness

While Jesus Christ alone has the power to save, He has given His children the power to witness to others about Him. You yourself must be a witness, and you must encourage others to be a witness through their words and deeds. In Matthew 28:19–20, when Jesus gave the Great Commission, His challenge to go and witness was for all Christians. Christian women can be powerful witnesses in their homes, their communities, and the world. But you must ask God to give you His power to witness.

My dad has always been a dynamic soul-winner. During his time away from the Lord, Dad says the thing he missed most was leading people to Jesus. When he returned to the Lord, he immediately began witnessing. Anytime you are with him, Dad tells others how to be saved. My dad often attributes his passion for soul-winning to two godly laymen who taught him boldness in witnessing when he was first saved. Their influence on him to witness has changed his life forever and changed the lives of others for eternity.

What do you understand the Bible to teach about the power to witness?

____

____

Read the following Scripture passages and summarize a biblical truth about witnessing from each passage. Scripture itself can empower you in your witness.

1 John 1:3 ______________________________________

____

Galatians 6:8 ___________________________________

____

Acts 1:8 _______________________________________

____

2 Corinthians 6:17 ______________________________

____

1 Peter 3:15 ____________________________________

____

Psalm 51:13 ____________________________________

____

1 Thessalonians 5:17 _____________________________

____

2 Timothy 1:7 ______________________________

____

In order to be a witness, a believer must have fellowship with Jesus Christ through a personal faith relationship (1 John 1:3). Secondly, a believer must have a love for others and a passion for the lost to be saved (Galatians 6:6–10).

In addition, believers must be willing to share the gospel with the whole world (Acts 1:8). A holy life, separated from the world, gives power to a believer's witness (2 Corinthians 6:17), and a word of witness brings salvation (1 Peter 3:15). A study of the Bible prepares the witness (Psalm 51:13), and unceasing prayer enables the witness (1 Thessalonians 5:17). God does not give fear to the believer. He gives power to witness (2 Timothy 1:7). The word of testimony plus a holy lifestyle give a believer the power to witness. This witness is the influence of holiness.

Power to Serve

The Holy Spirit gives us the power to witness and the power to serve. It is often service to others, specific acts of kindness, that influences an unbeliever to faith in Jesus Christ. A kind deed done in the name of Jesus can influence others to salvation and to holy living. While service is not necessary for salvation, service is an evidence of salvation. It is faith that saves, although works are a natural result of a right relationship with God.

In a final teaching to His disciples, Jesus discussed the judgment.

Read Matthew 25:31–46 to identify what determines how God will judge His people.

____

____

____

Salvation is based on faith alone, although the final judgment will be determined in part by the believer's treatment of others. Jesus said the sheep are those who serve others while the goats are those who serve self. Christ will separate the sheep from the goats. He will reward those who serve others in His name. Your acts of kindness do not go unnoticed by God.

Review Matthew 25:31–46 again to identify specific ways to serve others. What is the personal need, and how can you respond?

Their Need	My Response
Hungry	______
Thirsty	______
Stranger	______
Naked	______
Sick	______
Imprisoned	______

Who in your community has these needs? ______

The homeless population probably experiences these physical needs more than anyone else does. While I was teaching Girls in Action® (a missions education program) some years ago, a local missionary came to talk about her work. A photograph of a homeless man sleeping on a park bench made a powerful impression on those young girls. They couldn't imagine someone without a home or clothes or food. We quickly assembled some food bags to keep in our cars so that we could help the homeless when we saw them begging on a street corner. The missionary's commitment to serving those in need made a powerful impression on all of us. Service influences others to holiness.

Jesus challenges the believer to minister to others, but the Holy Spirit empowers us to serve. The Scripture teaches that as you meet the needs of others, you are ministering to Jesus Himself (Matthew 25:40). Often unselfish service gives your word of witness a voice—service influences others to holiness.

Power to Love

Jesus Christ gives to each believer the power to witness and the power to serve. He also gives to every believer the power to love. Love is definitely from God. Not only is God by His very nature love, but also He is the source of love. Love is God and love comes from God. Love expressed in words and actions definitely has the power to influence others. Your love can influence others to love.

Let's take a few moments to examine what the Scripture teaches about love, especially the power of love to change people. The story of the Samaritan woman recorded in John 4 summarizes the power of love. Jesus, in love, reached out to this sinful woman who had come to the well for water. He knew she needed more than water. She needed His love and eternal life. Because of His loving concern for her need, the woman accepted His gift of salvation. He not only gave her His unconditional love but also gave her the ability to love others.

Read John 4:27–30 to see the power of God's love in the life of the Samaritan woman. What happened as a result of her love for others?

____

____

____

Scripture records that this forgiven woman immediately began to tell others about Christ, and they were saved. Her personal testimony was a natural result of Christ's love for her and her love for others. Love motivates the believer to witness and serve. Love influences others to salvation and to holiness.

What is your personal testimony? What has God been doing in your life? How has God demonstrated His love to you? Write a brief testimony here and pray that God will use your testimony to influence others to Him.

My brother-in-law recently went with his young adult son on a missions trip to the Amazon River area of South America. The small group of believers took boats then canoes to obscure villages unreached by the gospel. As they performed medical and dental services, the missionary volunteers told the villagers about the love of Jesus. They explained that love motivated them to help people they did not know. More than 60 people including the chief were saved in one village alone. The power of God's love! And, don't you know that the love demonstrated in actions by a godly father had a profound influence on his son. More than words, our expressions of love can influence others to holiness.

God has given you the power to witness, to serve, and to love. His power can have a profound influence on people. His name alone can change the human heart and develop a holy life.

There is great power and influence in a name. My grandfather often reminded his young grandchildren to honor the family's name. He warned us that our actions could either strengthen or destroy the family's name. This is so true. A person's misbehavior can tarnish the family's name or her good conduct can honor the family's name. As Christians, our actions can also bring glory and honor or embarrassment and shame to our Father's name. A person's name can generate respect or ridicule based upon personal behavior. Reflect on the scorn shown toward Christianity when a believer stumbles in her faith or engages in immorality.

God desires for His name to be honored. The psalmist praised the greatness of God when he said, *"His name is holy and awe-inspiring"* (Psalm 111:9). God's name alone communicates love and respect.

Scripture also tells us *"that at the name of Jesus every knee should bow... and every tongue should confess that Jesus Christ is Lord, to the glory of God the Father"* (Philippians 2:10–11). There is power in the name of Jesus—power to save and power to change. That is why the holy life of a believer can influence others to Him. God's power to save and change is reflected through the holy lives of His children. Your one holy life can change the world!

Holy Scripture for Holy Living

Write the Scripture verse at the beginning of the chapter here. Then try to memorize it this week.

____

____

____

____

____

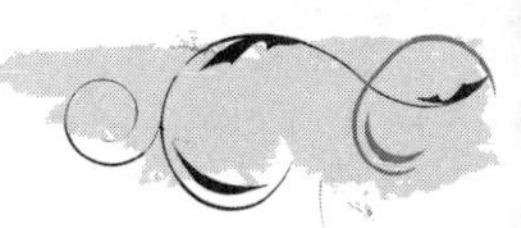

Practice Personal Holiness

What influence have you had on others? Has your one life made a difference for Him? Think of a person who has been influenced by you through your witness, your service, or your love. Write their names below.

My Witness ______________________________

____

____

My Service ______________________________

____

____

My Love ______________________________

____

____

Pray that God will continue to use you as an influence of holiness.

Lesson 12
The Longevity of Holiness

Revelation 4:8—*"Holy, holy, holy, Lord God, the Almighty, who was, who is, and who is coming."*

Now that we have studied what the Bible teaches about holiness, it is necessary for us to talk about the permanency of holiness. The Bible clearly states that God always has been and always will be holy. *"Holy, holy, holy, Lord God, the Almighty, who was, who is and who is coming"* (Revelation 4:8). His holiness is unchanging. And, God desires our holiness to be unchanging. He wants us to continue in holiness. He needs our holiness to be unchanging, to last forever—the longevity of holiness. If you believe that God's holiness is eternal and everlasting, then as a believer you must seek to maintain a holy lifestyle forever. That's the challenge in this unholy world!

It's easy for almost anyone to be holy for a moment, to be good for a time, to be godly while at church. The tough part of the Christian life is continuing in the faith and being holy day after day.

Is it hard for you to be persistent in living a holy life? Have you started to practice holy talking or holy actions and then stopped? Have you given up some bad habits to be more holy, then without even realizing it resumed those ungodly behaviors?

List below any commitments to holiness that you have made and broken.

____

____

____

Read Galatians 6:9 and 1 Corinthians 15:58 for encouragement. Now ask God's forgiveness. Then renew your commitment to continue in holiness for the rest of your life.

Let's consider the longevity of holiness. How long *does* and *should* holiness last? If we are speaking of the holiness of God, the answer is simple—God's holiness is eternal. But if we are considering human holiness, the answer is much more complex. Holiness in a believer should begin at conversion and continue through the process of sanctification. Holiness will be completed and continued during the time of glorification when we are present with the Father and absent from sin.

Humans must develop holiness before it can be sustained. Sinful human nature makes the consistency of holiness difficult. But by the Holy Spirit's power, any obedient believer can develop and maintain a holy life. Holiness by God's standard should last *a long time*. It should last for your lifetime as you daily recommit to holiness; it should last for your family's lifetime as you pass down a heritage of holiness; and it should last for all eternity as you experience purification in the presence of God.

Lasting for Your Lifetime

Holiness should last for a lifetime if it is genuine, if it is growing, and if it is glorifying God. Stephen Olford said, "Given spiritual life, holiness means the maintaining in health of that life before God and the setting apart of that life for His service alone." Though difficult and against human nature, holiness can last as you maintain that commitment to God every day of your life.

Read Revelation 4:1–11. Do you note in Isaiah 6:1–8 similarities between Isaiah's proclamation of the holiness of God and this proclamation by John?

Both passages talk about the glory and holiness of God. Both passages involve creatures in the proclamation. Both passages depict God on the throne. Both passages speak the word holy three times to stress its importance and longevity. These threefold proclamations also parallel the Trinity—Father, Son, and Holy Spirit.

In John's description of the throne of heaven, one can begin to imagine the glory and holiness of God. God's glory and holiness are everlasting.

What specific words or phrases from this passage depict the longevity of God's holiness?

John reinforced the longevity of God's holiness three times when he said they do not rest (v. 8), day and night (v. 8), and forever and ever (v. 10).

Evangelist Billy Graham has had a dynamic ministry for decades. Hundreds of thousands of people have come to know the Lord through his powerful preaching. But, Dr. Graham is also loved and admired because of his godly life and moral character.

His commitment to holiness in his personal life has definitely sustained his ministry. His longevity in holiness is a testimony of his unfaltering faith.

How can you maintain a holy life without resting, day and night, forever and ever? In one of his New Testament epistles, this same Apostle John gave directives for a lifetime of holiness. In 1 John 2:15–17, believers are warned not to love the world but to love God, not to long for the world but to desire God, not to live in the flesh but to follow the will of God. What a formula for lifelong holiness: love God, desire God, follow God. If you can make that commitment daily, then your holiness will last for a lifetime. In the same way, the creatures in Revelation 4:8–11 never stopped proclaiming the holiness of God, we should never stop living a holy life—without resting, day and night, forever and ever.

Lasting for Your Family's Lifetime

Holiness should last for your lifetime, but it should also be passed down through your family. There is no greater legacy than that of a holy life! Christian women have the command to be holy and the responsibility to teach holiness to others. The home is the perfect place for a lifestyle of holiness to be imitated and instructed. Wives, mothers, grandmothers, sisters, and aunts can pass along a spiritual heritage of holiness. On the other hand, if you are not maintaining holy living, your family will be less likely to develop and maintain holiness. An ungodly walk is obvious first to your family. You should be motivated to persevere in holiness for your own sake and the sake of your family.

The story of Lois and Eunice is an inspiring reminder of the power of a godly woman to influence her family to holiness.

Read 2 Timothy 1:3–5. How did Lois and Eunice teach young Timothy about holiness?

____

____

____

Timothy was grateful for the godly instruction of his grandmother Lois and his mother Eunice who taught him about faith, explained the Holy Scripture, and helped him increase in wisdom (see also 2 Timothy 3:15).

Are you grateful for the godly examples of your family?

What is your heritage of holiness?

Think of your own family tree. In the space below, fill in the names of those who passed along their faith and commitment to holiness.

Paternal Grandfather

Paternal Grandmother

Maternal Grandfather

Maternal Grandmother

Paternal Aunts/Uncles

Maternal Aunts/Uncles

Father

Mother

Sisters

Brothers

You ____________________

If you do not have a heritage of godly relatives, thank God that He has brought you into a relationship with Him. And, thank God for the many members of God's family who have invested in you spiritually.

Pray for your family members who do not know God. Briefly record how you will strive to change the heritage for those who come in generations after you.

Like Timothy, I am blessed with a godly heritage. My mother and both grandmothers were examples of holiness for me. I have a sister and aunts who are committed Christians. When I married, I inherited a godly family, a mother-in-law and four sisters-in-law who are dedicated believers. Of course, I should also mention all the men in my family who have continued our legacy of holiness. In full-time ministry and as committed laymen, the godly men in my family have influenced me. Now it is my turn to continue my family's heritage of faith. I have the responsibility of passing the faith and holiness down to our future generations.

Timothy had the responsibility to continue his personal holiness and to pass along that commitment to others. Paul affirmed the faith of Lois and Eunice, which was passed along to Timothy and in turn passed along to many others. Paul said, *"The churches were strengthened in the faith and were increased in number daily"* (Acts 16:5). You, too, have the opportunity and responsibility to pass your faith and holiness along to others. If you don't, holiness will not last for your family's lifetime.

While Chuck and I do not have children of our own, we still have a responsibility to pass along a lifestyle of holiness to the next generation. We have invested ourselves in the lives of our nieces and nephews with a desire for them to live godly lives. We have built special bonds with the children and now grandchildren of our friends in an effort to encourage their pursuits of holiness. We also have the privilege of influencing thousands of seminary children to walk and serve in holiness. Through us God's pattern for holiness shall continue.

To whom are you teaching faith and modeling holiness?

____

____

____

Name a few family members and friends whom you are influencing for God and godliness.

____

____

____

____

You will be a factor in the longevity of your family's holiness. You can be the torchbearer lighting the flame of holiness for the next generation. Holiness can be an heirloom passed along to future generations in your family.

For the believer, holiness lasts not only for a lifetime and through a legacy but also for all eternity. Holy living on earth is simply practice for an eternity of holiness with God in heaven. If the Christian doesn't enjoy being godly and seeking to be like God while alive on earth, that same Christian will be miserable in heaven where holiness is the norm not the exception. Can you imagine living in a place filled with only holy people for all eternity? What joy and satisfaction!

Lasting for All Eternity

In lesson 2, we discussed three doctrinal truths that explain salvation: *justification*, *sanctification*, and *glorification*. Do you remember the definitions? Let's review. *Justification* is experienced when a believer receives Jesus Christ as Savior and is saved from the penalty of sin that is death. *Sanctification* occurs during the believer's life as spiritual growth takes place and she is saved from the power of sin and enabled to live a holy life. *Glorification* comes after death when a believer becomes perfect like Christ and is saved from the presence of sin. It is in glorification that the believer's holiness can truly be complete and continue forever.

Let's take a few minutes to examine what a key Scripture teaches about glorification—that state of perfect holiness. Then we will learn how to continue growing in holiness until we are in the presence of God.

Read 1 Corinthians 15:50–58 and note at least three important truths about glorification.

____

____

____

____

____

____

What a joy to know that as a believer, one day I will be changed, incorruptible, and immortal in the presence of God! Death will be swallowed up by victory (1 Corinthians 15:54). That promise gives comfort to us personally and should motivate us to testify of this truth to others. The believer who dies is certainly in a better place and in a better state—with our Lord Jesus Christ, in perfect holiness.

It is exciting for a believer to consider being perfect like the Lord! In fact, it is somewhat unbelievable considering our sinfulness here on earth. But God promises that upon our death or His return, we will be perfect like Him and in the presence of Him in heaven.

What do you think of when you envision heaven? Describe heaven in your own words here.

You probably used many wonderful adjectives to describe the beauty of heaven, but don't forget the people of heaven. While heaven will have streets of gold and gates of pearl, the inhabitants of heaven will truly be the most welcome sight. God, the Holy One, will be sitting on His throne with all the heavenly hosts around Him. Believers from across the ages will enjoy fellowship with the Father. And you, dear believer, will be in the midst of them, in your most holy state, to spend all eternity.

Yes, the Bible tells us about heaven—the place prepared by God for all believers (John 14:3). The Bible teaches that heaven is a place without sorrow or sin. In heaven there will be no tears and no pain. (Read Revelation 21:1–7 for a true glimpse of heaven.) And in heaven, for the first time in our lives, we will be like Christ—perfect in every way. We will live in His presence forever. But heaven and glorification come later. For the believer, it is most important to develop holiness now.

The key to longevity in holiness is perseverance. Perseverance is the ability to continue—to go on living a holy life, day after day. Once you have committed to holy living, you must make a daily recommitment to holiness. As Paul concluded in 1 Corinthians 15, you must be *"steadfast, immovable, always excelling in the Lord's work, knowing that your labor in the Lord is not in"* (1 Corinthians 15:58). If you continue in holiness, then you will be able to stand before the

Lord in heaven knowing that you have grown in your likeness of Him. And at that moment, you will truly be like Him! Holiness is a Christian virtue worthy of sustaining and worthy of proclaiming.

Holy Scripture for Holy Living

Write the Scripture verse at the beginning of the chapter here. Then try to memorize it this week.

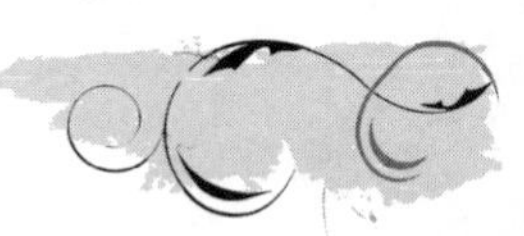

Practice Personal Holiness

God's plan for the believer is a life of holiness that will last. How long has holiness lasted in your life and in your family? How long will you live a holy life? Reflect on your own life and the lives of your family members.

Write a one-sentence testimony or commitment of the longevity of your own holiness as well as the holiness of your family and for all eternity.

As you write, renew your commitment to be steadfast and immovable in your holiness.

My Lifetime of Holiness ________________________________

____

____

My Family's Lifetime of Holiness ________________________

____

____

My Eternal Lifetime of Holiness__________________________

____

____

Conclusion

What has God taught you about holiness? Are you putting His principles into practice? Is your life a reflection of His character and conduct? It is my prayer that this 12-week Bible study has been both convicting and convincing. The Holy Spirit does the convicting of sin and sinfulness while His Word does the convincing of His power to redeem and transform. What has been your response? Are you leading a life of personal holiness? Have you made holiness a lifelong commitment?

During the writing of this study, I received a letter of confession from a friend in the ministry. He was asking for his family and his friends to forgive him for his failure. Because of personal immorality, he lost his marriage, his family, and his church. He had just realized the devastation of his sin. His pain and remorse were so apparent in his writing.

While God promises him forgiveness, my friend will experience the consequences of his sin for a long time. How can sin like that be prevented? How can other Christians avoid that mistake? We will stand up to temptation only with the help of the Holy Spirit and commitment to personal holiness. You may feel immune from immorality or separated from sinfulness. But remember your own sinful nature and the power of the evil one. Satan is prowling around looking for Christians he can devour. So be alert! Be on guard! Resist him! And keep your eyes fixed on Jesus. Determine daily to live a holy life. Only then will you be holy like God and receive His abundant blessings. A. W. Tozer said it like this: "The holy man is not one who cannot sin. A holy man is one who will not sin." It is critical for Christians today to avoid sin and seek holiness. There is no greater blessing or testimony than a holy life.

Let's discuss a few practical suggestions as you conclude this study. I would recommend that you practice these holy habits daily.

While you may think of some other principles for holiness, these suggestions may help you live for Him for the rest of your life.

1. Praise and adore your Holy God regularly.
2. Understand that we are to be His holy people.
3. Accept His call for personal holiness.
4. Revere some holy heroes in the Word and the world.
5. Develop a character and conduct of holiness.
6. Pray diligently for the unholy people in this unholy world.
7. Develop daily holiness in your words and deeds.
8. Replace unholy habits with holy habits.
9. Pursue a life of holiness faithfully.
10. Enjoy the blessings of holiness.
11. Allow God to use your holiness to influence others.
12. Be holy now, through your legacy, and for all eternity.

And remember, holiness brings far more joy than sinfulness could ever give you. Don't be tantalized by temporary thrills; experience true joy through a lifelong commitment to holiness.

Now you may ask: *what next? What should I do now that I have completed this Bible study on holiness?* The answer is simple to say but difficult to do. Persevere. Continue. Keep on. *Persevere* in your study of holiness. *Continue* to be holy in all your thoughts and actions. *Keep on* challenging others to become holy through your own words and example. If you keep on doing these things, you will be called *holy*. This is the commitment I make to God and this is the commitment I make to you, dear friend. I commit myself to living a holy life every day from now on. Do you make that commitment? I pray that your commitment to holiness is sincere and strong. I will pray for you and will covet your prayers for me. Many blessings as you live out this holy life!

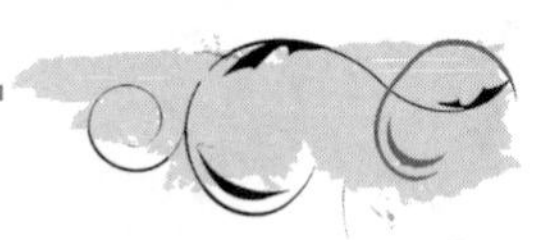

Wholly Holy

Be holy, for I am holy;
Be godly, for I am God.

Holy Father
Holy Son
Holy Spirit
Three in One.

Holy in being
Holy in love
Holy in life
He reigns above.

Wholly holy, He alone
Is truly holy, the Righteous One.
Because we are His
And His power is ours
We can be holy
Wholly holy
His power is ours.

—Rhonda H. Kelley

For Further Thought

"Holiness is inwrought by the Holy Spirit, not because we have suffered, but because we have surrendered."

—Richard Shelley Taylor

"How little people know who think that holiness is dull. When one meets the real thing. . . it is irresistible."

—C. S. Lewis

"If but ten among us lead a holy life, we shall kindle a fire which shall light up the entire city."

—St. John Chrysostom

"The greatest miracle that God can do today is to take an unholy man out of an unholy world, and make that man holy and put him back into that unholy world and keep him holy in it."

—Leonard Ravenhill

"It might be well if we stopped using the terms victory and defeat to describe our progress in holiness. Rather we should use the terms obedience and disobedience."

—Jerry Bridges

"Holiness is not freedom from temptation, but power to overcome temptation."

—G. Campbell Morgan

"There are no shortcuts to maturity. It takes time to be holy."

—Erwin W. Lutzer

"Saying yes to God means saying no to things that offend His holiness."

—A. Morgan Derham

"Joy not only results from a holy life, but there is also a sense in which joy helps produce a holy life."

—Jerry Bridges

"Holiness is the walk of faith in the life of progressive sanctification made possible in us by the Holy Spirit through obedience to the Word of God."

—Charles F. Stanley

"Given spiritual life, holiness means the maintaining in health of that life before God and the setting apart of that life for His service alone."

—Stephen F. Olford

"The destined end of man is not happiness, nor health, but holiness."

—Oswald Chambers

"Holiness does not consist in mystic speculations, enthusiastic fervors, or uncommanded austerities; it consists in thinking as God thinks and will as God wills."

—Chuck Colson

"The holy man is not one who cannot sin. A holy man is one who will not sin."

—A. W. Tozer

"The beauty of holiness has done more, and will do more to regenerate the world than all that has ever been preached or written on Christianity."

—Thomas Chalmers

"A holy life is a voice; it speaks when the tongue is silent, and is either a constant attraction or a perpetual reproof."

—Robert Leighton

"Holiness is inwrought by the Holy Spirit, not because we have suffered, but because we have surrendered."

—Richard Shelley Taylor

"A holy life is not an ascetic, or gloomy, or solitary life, but a life regulated by divine truth and faithful in Christian duty."

— Tyron Edwards

"Let no man think himself to be holy because he is not tempted, for the holiest and highest in life have the most temptations."

—John Wycliffe

Scriptures About Holiness

Old Testament

Exodus 3:5
Exodus 15:11
Exodus 20:8
Leviticus 19:2
Deuteronomy 7:6
1 Samuel 2:2
2 Chronicles 30:27
Psalm 2:6
Psalm 89:35
Psalm 93:5
Psalm 99:9
Psalm 111:9
Psalm 145:21
Isaiah 6:3
Isaiah 30:15
Isaiah 35:8

New Testament

Mark 6:20
Luke 1:6
Luke 4:34
Romans 1:2
Romans 6:22
Romans 12:1–2
2 Corinthians 7:1
Ephesians 1:4
Ephesians 4:24
Colossians 3:12
1 Thessalonians 3:13
1 Thessalonians 4:7
1 Timothy 2:8
2 Timothy 1:9
Hebrews 12:10, 14
1 Peter 1:15–16
1 Peter 2:9
1 John 2:15–17
Revelation 4:8
Revelation 15:4
Revelation 21:2
Revelation 22:11

Group Teaching Guide

This section includes some teaching suggestions for the small group leader. It also provides a format for the discussion time and a typical schedule for a one-hour session. A focus group has tried this particular approach, and it was successful. Let the Holy Spirit lead your group discussion, and make any appropriate changes. These are simply teaching helps.

Lesson 1: A Holy God

Prayertime (5 minutes)

Ask each participant to write a prayer of commitment in the front of her Bible study book. Spend a few minutes in personal prayer, asking God to bless this Bible study.

Review (5 minutes)

Discuss the weekly format for this study and give details about the group meeting. Encourage each member to complete her own study before discussing it with the group.

Introduction (5 minutes)

Ask the group to call out synonyms for the word *holy*. Encourage and accept all words that reflect a biblical or a worldview of holiness. Write these words on a board so that everyone can see them.

Group Discussion (40 minutes)

1. Discuss the literal meaning of the word *holy*. Go back to the words listed in the introduction and look up additional definitions in

other dictionaries. Discuss definitions that are distortions of the true meaning and those that are accurate perceptions of true holiness.

2. Read Isaiah 6:1–8 aloud. Have participants describe the holiness of God. Encourage them to focus more on His character than His creation.

3. Discuss the sinless nature of God as described in Psalm 89:30–37. Ask participants to suggest words to describe sinless (holy, spotless, without blemish, righteous, etc.).

4. Have participants share times when God has revealed His glory and holiness to them.

Closing (5 minutes)

1. Sing together the chorus "Our God Is an Awesome God."

2. Respond to God's revelation of His holiness. Enter into a time of praise, asking participants to call out words that describe the holy character of God. Close the prayertime by reading this week's Holy Scripture for Holy Living (Isaiah 6:3) aloud together.

Lesson 2: A Holy People

Prayertime (5 minutes)

Give an index card to each member and ask her to record one specific prayer request. Collect the cards. Then distribute one card to each person. Pray silently for that particular need and continue praying about that specific concern all week.

Review (5 minutes)

Review Lesson One by asking the following questions:

What is holiness?

How should we respond to the holiness of God?
Has God revealed anything new to you this week about His holiness?

Introduction (5 minutes)

Ask participants to reminisce about the children's game "follow the leader." What were the rules of the game? What made it fun? What made it challenging? Sometimes the leader in the game purposely performs acts that come easily to her, but will be difficult for her followers—that is the challenge! God is our leader and we are to follow Him. Holiness seems natural for God, but impossible for us—His followers. Explain that the difference between the childhood game and following God in holiness is that instead of trying to "put us out," God actually empowers us to follow Him successfully.

Group Discussion (40 minutes)

1. Read 1 Peter 1:13–21 and ask: *Why are believers to be holy?*

2. Discuss the biblical teachings about God's call. Encourage participants to share testimonies of God's call in their lives.

3. Discuss specific guidelines for holy conduct as given in Leviticus 19. Ask participants to suggest how they can follow those guidelines today.

4. Read Matthew 4:18–22; 26:39; and John 8:8–12. Discuss the call and the commitment made in each of these passages.

Closing (5 minutes)

1. Read this week's Holy Scripture for Holy Living (1 Peter 1:15–16) aloud together.

2. Ask each member to find the person in the group for whom she prayed as the class began. Pray for their specific request and for their commitment to holiness. Allow time for this prayer before closing with a prayer for holy conduct among believers.

Prayertime (5 minutes)

Open the study with a silent time of prayer. Lead participants in asking God to confirm His holiness, convict them of their sinfulness, and call them to lives of holiness.

Lesson 3: A Life of Holiness

Review (5 minutes)

Review previous lessons by asking:

1. What thoughts have you had this week regarding God and His holiness?

2. What does the Scripture teach about holy living?

Introduction (5 minutes)

Ask the participants of the class, When you were children, what did you want to be when you grew up? Did any women in the group actually fulfill those early desires? Introduce the idea of "growing up" into holiness.

Group Discussion (40 minutes)

1. Read 1 Thessalonians 4:1–8 and discuss the Christian's call to holy living. Be sure to cover *"walk in God,"* (v. 1) *"please God,"* (v. 1), *"do so even more,"* (v. 1) and *"possess your own vessel in sanctification and honor"* (v. 4).

2. Read Romans 12:1–2, and discuss God's will for the believer. Contrast the phrase be transformed with be conformed.

3. Ask participants to answer the question: What pleases you? Read Philippians 4:8–9, Colossians 3:20, and Hebrews 13:21. Identify the things that please God.

4. Answer the question: How are you living out God's call to a holy life?

Closing (5 minutes)

1. Read this week's Holy Scripture for Holy Living (1 Thessalonians 4:7) aloud together.

2. Have a time of prayer asking God to reveal to each member ways in which she has pleased Him. Ask participants to pray silently, renewing their commitment to please God through holy living.

Lesson 4: Holy Heroes

Prayertime (5 minutes)

Follow this model for prayer as participants of your group voice sentence prayers to the Father.
A — adoration
C— confession
T— thanksgiving
S— supplication

Review (5 minutes)

Review the previous lessons by asking:

1. Who is called to be holy?

2. Why are Christians to be holy?

Introduction (5 minutes)

Ask participants, Who is your hero? Why? Whom do you look up to because of their character and contributions? Accept heroes from all areas of life. Then direct the discussion toward biblical heroes.

Group Discussion (40 minutes)

1. Read Luke 1:5–6. Discuss the heroic attribute of righteousness as displayed by Elizabeth. Discuss other righteous heroes and talk about what is involved in heroic righteousness.

2. Read Luke 2:36–38. Discuss the heroic attribute of service as displayed by Anna. Discuss other servant heroes and talk about what is involved in heroic servanthood.

3. Read Luke 10:38–42. Discuss the heroic attribute of commitment as displayed by Mary of Bethany. Discuss other committed heroes and talk about what is involved in heroic commitment.

4. Read the quote from Corrie ten Boom. Make two columns on the board, and title them *Command* and *Provision*. In the command column, write: *Love your enemies.* In the provision column, write: *the love itself.* Ask the women to name other commands God gives us, and what His provision is for keeping them.

Closing (5 minutes)

1. Read this week's Holy Scripture for Holy Living (Luke 1:6) aloud together.

2. Have a participant take each of the commands written on the board, and pray a sentence prayer for the other participants that they would walk in that commandment, and be holy, like Elizabeth, Anna, and Mary of Bethany.

Lesson 5: Developing Holiness

Prayertime (5 minutes)

Ask participants to pray in "prayer triplets" (groups of three). Pray specifically for each person to be "built up in Christ."

Review (5 minutes)

Review the previous lessons by asking:

1. *What are some characteristics of holy heroes?*

2. *Have you encountered any holy heroes this week?*

Introduction (5 minutes)

Read the three-part definition of process given in the lesson. Have participants name some processes in which they are involved (for example: redecorating a house, getting a college degree, adopting a baby, etc.). Discuss how life itself is a series of processes.

Group Discussion (40 minutes)

1. Begin the discussion by asking, *What does it mean to be sanctified?* Develop a working definition of the word *sanctification*.

2. Read Colossians 2:20–23. Discuss the things the world turns to for sanctification.

3. Read Leviticus 20:8. Who sanctifies us?

4. Discuss the process of sanctification as described in Colossians 3:1–14.

5. Make three columns on the board with headings: *Put to Death, Take Off, Put On*. Have participants list items in each column from the passage in Colossians 3.

6. Discuss the process of getting dressed. Point out to the class that we cannot put on a new set of clothes until we have shed the old set.

Closing (5 minutes)

1. Read this week's Holy Scripture for Holy Living (Col. 3:12) aloud together.

2. Have a time of silent prayer, asking the participants to pray for the person on their left that they would take off ungodliness, then for the person on their right that they would put on godliness. Close this time of prayer by singing together "Take Time to be Holy."

Lesson 6: An Unholy World

Prayertime (5 minutes)

Spend time praying these Scriptures about holiness: 1 Peter 1:15–16; 1 Thessalonians 4:7; Luke 1:6; Colossians 3:12. Voice these Scriptures aloud and personalize them with the name of a member of the class.

Review (5 minutes)

Review the previous lessons by asking:

1. *What do we know about the holiness of God?*

2. *What do we know about the holiness of God's people?*

Introduction (5 minutes)

Distribute copies of a local newspaper, including all sections, to the participants of the class. Have them skim the headlines of their sections for comments on the unholiness of the world in which we live. Point out that this is not a new phenomenon, that the world has been unholy since sin first entered the world.

Group Discussion (40 minutes)

1. Read 1 John 2:15–17. Discuss temptation, the tempter, and the result of temptation as described in Scripture.

2. Read Ephesians 6:10–17. Discuss how the believer is able to resist temptation.

3. Contrast the terms *testing* and *temptation*. Stress that testing comes from God, while temptations come from Satan. Based on 1 John 2:3–11, discuss the ways a believer is tested. Stress that God can use both temptation and testing to strengthen the believer's faith.

4. Discuss the believer's triumph over testing and temptation as described in Romans 8:2; John 8:34–36; John 8:31–32; Romans 5:9; Galatians 5:13–14; and Romans 6:23. If time permits, ask participants to read each reference aloud.

Closing (5 minutes)

1. Read aloud together this week's Holy Scripture for Holy Living (1 John 2:15).

2. Pray, asking God to reveal to each participant aspects of this world she loves. Ask Him to help her turn away from those temptations and turn toward Him for holiness.

Lesson 7: Daily Holiness

Prayertime (5 minutes)

Write the following topics on index cards and give to six participants: *Praise to God*, *Participants of Bible study group*, *The church*, *Christian friends*, *Unsaved friends*, and *Thanksgiving to God*. Ask each participant to voice a topical sentence prayer.

Review (5 minutes)

Review previous lessons briefly by asking these questions:

1. *Who calls us to be holy?*

2. *Who tempts us to unholiness?*

3. *Who gives us triumph and enables us to be holy?*

Introduction (5 minutes)

Read Steve Martini's quote, "The trouble most people have resisting temptation is that they never really want to discourage it completely." Discuss the requirement of total commitment in becoming holy.

Group Discussion (40 minutes)

1. Discuss the Scriptures listed in this lesson that instruct Christians as to daily conduct (Psalm 61:8; 72:15; 88:9; Isaiah 58:2, etc.). What does it mean to make a daily commitment to holiness?

2. Discuss the meaning of dedication. Have participants describe people they know who are truly dedicated. Make a list on the board of behaviors that participants mention that indicate dedication.

3. Discuss the meaning of discipline. Discuss the difference in divine discipline and human discipline.

4. Have the participants list spiritual disciplines that are necessary for daily holiness. Discuss the importance of each one.

Closing (5 minutes)

1. Read aloud together this week's Holy Scripture for Holy Living (Luke 9:23).

2. Have participants form pairs, share one specific goal in a spiritual discipline, and pray together for the dedication to reach their goals.

Lesson 8: Holy Habits

Prayertime (5 minutes)
Ask each person to find a prayer partner and spend time praying in this manner: Praise to God, Petition for Others, Prayer for Self.

Review (5 minutes)

Pose these questions: *Has God convicted you of unholiness during this study? Have you made a genuine commitment to holy living? Would you share some specific things you have learned?*

Introduction (5 minutes)

Introduce this lesson by mentioning our nation's obsession with youth. Have participants list habits that we pursue energetically in order to maintain an appearance of youth. Guide participants to list habits that will make us look older. Discuss the principles of holiness given from Jerry Bridges' *The Pursuit of Holiness* but in the context of maintaining that youthful appearance. Relate this discussion to the spiritual concept of the old man in sin and the new man in Christ. Say that we want our habits to indicate that we are new in Christ rather than old women!

Group Discussion (40 minutes)

1. Make two columns on the board with the headings: *Old* and *New*. From Ephesians 4:17–32, compare and contrast the old man in sin with the new man in Christ.

2. Discuss holy habits that believers should develop through frequent repetition as suggested in this week's lesson.

3. Have participants share with the group any other holy habits they would want to add to this list. How will they develop these holy habits?

Closing (5 minutes)

1. Read this week's Holy Scripture for Holy Living (Ephesians 4:24) aloud together.
2. Pray, asking God to create in each participant a new person of true righteousness and holiness. As the group leader, pray specifically this week for each member of your group to develop holy habits.

Lesson 9: The Pursuit of Holiness

Prayertime (5 minutes)

Begin this group session with a directed quiet time. Ask participants to pray silently following this model that you have written on the board:

Praise to God
Confession of Sin
Requests for Self (physical needs, mental needs, spiritual needs)
Confidence in God

Review (5 minutes)

Review the previous lesson by asking these questions:

1. *What do we need to do in order to become holy?*

2. *What have been some stumbling blocks to your pursuit of personal holiness?*

Introduction (5 minutes)

Ask participants to list things that we actively pursue (examples: an academic degree, physical fitness, a sales bargain). Read Hebrews 12:14, and ask if we pursue holiness with the same zeal with which we pursue other goals.

Group Discussion (40 minutes)

1. Read Isaiah 6:1–8. Reflect on the posture of the seraphim as they beheld the holiness of God. In three columns on the board, write: *Covered face—Reverence, Covered feet—Humility,* and *Flying—Service.* Discuss what each means then list in each column ways to live out the reverence, humility, and service demonstrated by the seraphim.

2. Discuss the meaning of reverence. Discuss Mary of Bethany's demonstration of reverence and the ways that we can demonstrate the same attitude of honor and respect.

3. Discuss how humility flows naturally from reverence. Discuss God's response to the humble and how His response is dramatically different from the world's view of humility.

4. Discuss the relationship of service to holy living. *According to the Scriptures listed in this section, what is the motivation for service that is holy?*

Closing (5 minutes)

1. Read this week's Holy Scripture for Holy Living (Hebrews 12:14) aloud together.

2. Reflect on the many ways believers should wholeheartedly pursue holiness. Holiness reflected upward is seen in a reverence for God; holiness reflected inward is seen in humility of self; and holiness reflected outward is seen in service to others.

Lesson 10: The Fruit of Holiness

Prayertime (5 minutes)

As participants come in, ask them to find Psalm 23 and spend time meditating on this prayer of David.

Review (5 minutes)

To review previous lessons, ask participants to share reasons for and results of a pursuit of holiness.

Introduction (5 minutes)

Ask participants to list some examples of "the fruit of our labor" (examples may include: money, clean house, well–behaved children, a meal, etc.) This is a worldly idiom, so reflect further on "fruit" in the Bible (examples may include: the command to be fruitful and multiply, the fruit in the Garden of Eden, Fruit of the Spirit, Jesus' command to bear fruit, etc.). Challenge participants to search for types of biblical fruit and offer a prize to the first person to identify "Fruit Loops" in this lesson. (Fruit Loops refers to the circular nature in the production of fruit: the development of holiness produces fruit, the fruit leads to becoming more holy, which leads to more fruit, etc.). Have an elaborately wrapped box of Fruit Loops cereal to award to the winner.

Group Discussion (40 minutes)

1. Have individuals read aloud Philippians 1:11; James 3:18; Romans 1:13; 1 Corinthians 16:15; and John 4:36. Based on these verses, develop a group definition of *fruit*.

2. Read Galatians 5:22–23. Have participants name ways that each aspect of the Fruit of the Spirit is manifested in their lives.

3. Focus on joy, and discuss the difference between joy and happiness. Discuss sources of joy and talk about what robs us of joy (John 15:10–11 and Psalm 51:8,12).

4. Discuss the meaning of wisdom. Read James 3:13–18 and discuss the difference between heavenly wisdom and earthly wisdom.

5. Discuss the relationship of freedom and holiness according to Romans 6:22. How can we understand this biblical truth, which seems so opposite from human reason?

6. Discuss how the fruit of holiness will be seen in a believer's worship, walk, and work.

Closing (5 minutes)

1. Read this week's Holy Scripture for Holy Living (Romans 6:22) aloud together.

2. If no one has identified Fruit Loops, explain the concept of the circular nature in the production of fruit.

3. Close the study in prayer, thanking God for a fruitful group of believers.

Lesson 11: The Influence of Holiness

Prayertime (5 minutes)

For today's prayertime, slowly and prayerfully say together The Lord's Prayer (Matthew 6:9–13).

Review (5 minutes)

Review previous lessons by asking:

How do we experience joy in personal holiness, when the world sometimes views it as boring or strange?

Introduction (5 minutes)

Ask the women in your group to list things that influenced how they dressed today (ex: the weather, lunch plans, what was clean, etc.). Ask them to name people who have had a profound influence on their lives (encourage both negative and positive examples). Conclude your introduction by discussing the power of influence.

Group Discussion (40 minutes)

1. Discuss the relationship between power and influence.

2. From the Scripture given in the lesson, how does our personal holiness empower us to witness?

3. Have someone read aloud Matthew 25:31–46. Discuss how God will judge His people who do not serve Him and others. On the board, make two columns. In the first, list the specific needs identified in this passage. In the second, list specific ways your group is serving or can begin serving the needy.

4. Discuss the power of Jesus's love for the Samaritan woman as described in John 4:27–30. Ask participants to contemplate how they have experienced the power of His love in their own lives.

5. Read 1 John 4:7–21. Ask participants to identify why and how believers are to love one another. Ask if they are ever afraid to love others. Offer verses 17 and 18 as the supernatural answer to this natural fear. Emphasize that loving our brother (or sister) is a command (v. 21) and that God empowers us to keep His commands.

6. Take time to share brief testimonies of Christians who have been influential in participants' lives.

7. Discuss challenges of sharing our faith and being a witness.

Closing (5 minutes)

1. Read aloud together this week's Holy Scripture for Holy Living (Psalm 111:9).

2. Pray that your group's witness, service, and love will reflect God's holiness to the world.

Lesson 12: The Longevity of Holiness

Prayertime (5 minutes)

Today's opening prayer will be for unbelievers. Suggest that each person write down the name of one unsaved friend then spend time praying for that person's salvation. Ask God to help your holy life be a witness to your lost friends and family participants.

Review (5 minutes)

Review previous lessons by asking questions about holiness (for example: *Who is holy? What is holiness? Where are we holy? When did we become holy? Why are we holy?* etc.).

Introduction (5 minutes)

Continue asking "wh–" questions. Ask, *when did God become holy? When will He stop being holy?* Illustrate the importance of longevity by asking your group about the length of things like movies, diets, marriages, books, time at college, sermons, and so forth. Mention that we often judge the value of things by their length. Some things are better if they are longer, while others are better if they are shorter. Point out that it is not the length of time, but its length of influence that matters. We can further understand holiness as we look at its longevity. God has always been holy. God will always be holy.

Group Discussion (40 minutes)

1. Have one part of the group look up and read Isaiah's proclamation of God's holiness in Isaiah 6:1–8 and another part of the group look up and read Revelation 4:1–11. Identify phrases that refer to the longevity of God's holiness.

2. Read 1 John 2:15–17 aloud. Ask participants to point out what will pass away and what will last forever. Discuss how this is a key to holiness that will last a lifetime.

3. Discuss the heritage that Timothy received from Lois and Eunice. Ask participants to share from their own heritage. Because it is likely that there will be women in your group who do not have a family heritage of holiness, ask also for participants to share about someone in their background who "passed the faith" along to them.

4. Review the doctrinal truths of justification, sanctification, and glorification. Ask participants to share the truths about glorification seen in 1 Corinthians 15:50–58.

5. Read 1 Corinthians 15:58 aloud. Discuss the things that cause us to move from the path of holiness and make us tire in the work of the Lord. Read the verse again in another version as an encouragement that our "labor is not in vain."

Closing (5 minutes)

1. Ask participants to share what they have learned about holiness in this study.

2. Ask for practical suggestions they have or intend to incorporate in order to become holy.

3. Close with a prayer for participants to continue in their study and pursuit of holiness. Close your prayer by reading or saying this week's Holy Scripture for Holy Living (Revelation 4:8) aloud together.

Answers to Direct Questions

This section will provide specific answers to direct questions in each lesson. The responses were compiled from Scripture and other biblical sources. Some of the questions solicit personal perspective, so there is no one correct answer. These answers are not included. A key is provided to give you additional insights into personal holiness.

Lesson 1: A Holy God

Based on Psalm 89:30–37, describe the sinless character of God (fill in blanks): *faithful love, faithfulness, covenant, have said, holiness, lie.*

Lesson 5: Developing Holiness

From Colossians 3:5, list some of the sins that should no longer be a part of the believer's life: *sexual immorality, impurity, lust, evil desire, greed idolatry.*

From Colossians 3:8–9, list the acts of ungodliness Paul says to take off (personal examples not included here): *anger, wrath, malice, slander, filthy language, lying.*

Lesson 7: Daily Holiness

Daily lessons from Scripture:
Psalm 61:8—*fulfilling my vows day by day*
Psalm 72:15—*pray continually, and praise spiritual leaders*
Psalm 88: 8–9—*cry out to the Lord all day long*

Isaiah 58:2—*seek God day after day, know His ways, delight in the nearness of God*
Mark 14:49—*be in His presence every day, teach His Word daily*
Luke 9:23—*come after Him, deny self, take up His cross daily, follow Him daily*
Acts 2:46–47—*devote selves daily to gathering and breaking bread, praising God and adding those being saved*
Acts 17:11—*study the Bible daily, make daily application*
Hebrews 3:13—*encourage each other daily, so that none of you will sin*
Hebrews 10:11—*minister day after day and offer sacrifices daily*

Lesson 8: Holy Habits

Holy habits from Scripture (fill in the blank):

1. *steal, deceptively or lie*
2. *obey, commands and statutes*
3. *reverential awe*
4. *treasure*
5. *truth*
6. *idle, diligent*
7. *enemies, pray*
8. *others, you*
9. *commands*
10. *teaching, fellowship, breaking of bread, prayers*
11. *sexual immorality, body*
12. *patient, kind, not envy, not boastful, not conceited*
13. *neighbor, yourself*
14. *good*
15. *forgive, forgave*
16. *careful*
17. *strong*
18. *joy*
19. *thoughts*
20. *walk, thankfulness*
21. *encourage*
22. *prayer*
23. *generous*
24. *ashamed*
25. *complain*

Lesson 9: The Pursuit of Holiness

How God rewards the humble (fill in the blank):
exalts, lift, due

Lesson 10: The Fruit of Holiness

Heavenly wisdom is:

pure, peace-loving, gentle, compliant, full of mercy, full of good fruits, no favoritism, no hypocrisy

Earthly wisdom is:

bitter envy, selfish ambition, disorder, every kind of evil

Bibliography

Abraham, Ken. *Positive Holiness.* Old Tappan, NJ: Fleming H. Revell, 1988.

Allen, Catherine B. *The New Lottie Moon Story.* Nashville: Broadman Press, 1980.

Baxter, J. Sidlow. *A New Call to Holiness.* Grand Rapids, MI: Zondervan Publishing House, 1967.

Brengle, Samuel Logan. *Heart Talks on Holiness.* London: Salvationist Publishing and Supplies, 1897.

Bridges, Jerry. *The Pursuit of Holiness*. Colorado Springs: NavPress, 1978.

Bridges, Jerry. *The Pursuit of Holiness—Study Guide*. Colorado Springs: NavPress, 1978.

Craig, Sheila. *A Woman's Journey Toward Holiness*. Wheaton, IL: Crossway Books, 1997.

Drury, Keith. *Holiness for Ordinary People*. Grand Rapids, MI: Francis Asbury, Press, 1983.

Dunning, H. Ray. *Grace, Faith, and Holiness*. Kansas City, MO: Beacon Hill Press of Kansas City, 1988.

Fenhagen, James C. *Invitation to Holiness*. San Francisco: Harper and Row Publishers, 1985.

Foster, Richard J. *Celebration of Discipline: The Path to Spiritual Growth*. San Francisco: Harper & Row, 1988.

Hauerwas, Stanley. *Sanctify Them in the Truth: Holiness Exemplified*. Nashville, TN: Abingdon Press, 1998.

Holman Bible Dictionary. Nashville: Holman Bible Publishers, 1991.

Ironside, H. A. *Holiness: The False and the True*. New York: Loizeaux Brothers, Inc., 1953.

Kelley, Rhonda H. *Divine Discipline: How to Develop and Maintain Self-Control*. Gretna, LA: Pelican Publishing Company, 1992.

___. *Life Lessons from Women in the Bible*. Nashville: LifeWay Press, 1998.

___. *A Woman's Guide to Spiritual Wellness: A Personal Study of Colossians*. Birmingham, AL: New Hope Publishers, 1998.

Koeberle, Adolf. *The Quest for Holiness*. St. Louis: Concordia Press, 1982.

Larsen, Earnest. *Holiness*. New York: Paulist Press, 1975.

Martin, Steve. Compelling Evidence. New York: The Berkley Publishing Group.

McClung, Floyd. *Holiness and the Spirit of the Age*. Eugene, OR: Harvest House Publishers, 1990.

Merriam–Webster's Collegiate Dictionary. Springfield, MA: Merriam-Webster, 1997.

Moore, Beth. *Living Beyond Yourself: Exploring the Fruit of the Spirit*. Nashville: Lifeway Press, 1998.

Morgan, Hugh D. *The Holiness of God and His People*. Wales: Evangelical Press of Wales, 1979.

Morgan, John. *Holiness Acceptable to God*. Minneapolis: Bethany House Publishers, 1986.
Murray, Andrew. *The Believer's Secret of Holiness*. Minneapolis: Bethany House Publishers, 1984.

Neill, Stephen. *Christian Holiness*. London: Lutterworth Press, 1960.

Olford, Stephen F. *The Way of Holiness*. Wheaton, IL: Crossway Books, 1998.

Packer, J. I. *Knowing God*. Downers Grove, IL: InterVarsity Press, 1993.

Parsons, Martin. *The Call to Holiness*. Grand Rapids, MI: William B. Eerdmans Publishing Company, 1974.

Patterson, Dorothy Kelley, and Rhonda Harrington Kelley, eds. *Women's Evangelical Commentary: New Testament*. Nashville: Broadman and Holman Publishers, 2006.

Prior, Kenneth. *The Way of Holiness*. Downers Grove, IL: InterVarsity Press, 1973.

Reed, Gerard. *C. S. Lewis and the Bright Shadow of Holiness*. Kansas City, MO: Beacon Hill Press of Kansas City, 1999.

Roseveare, Helen. *Living Holiness*. Minneapolis: Bethany House Publishers, 1986.

Ryle, J. C. *Holiness*. London: James Clarke & Co., 1952.

Smith, Hannah Whitall. The christian's secret of a Happy Life. Westwood, NJ: barbour and Company, Inc., 1985.

Sproul, R. C. *The Holiness of God*. Wheaton, IL: Tyndale House Publishers, 1985.

Sproul, R. C. *Pleasing God*. Wheaton, IL: Tyndale House Publishers, 1988.

Tada, Joni Eareckson. *Holiness in Hidden Places*. Dallas: Word Books, 1999.

Ten Boom, Corrie. *The Hiding Place*. Washington Depot, CT: Chosen Books, 1971.

Tracy, Wesley D. et al. *The Upward Call: Spiritual Formation and the Holy Life*. Kansas City, MO: Beacon Hill of Kansas City, 1994.

Trevethan, Thomas L. T*he Beauty of God's Holiness*. Downers Grove, IL: InterVarsity Press, 1995.

White, John. *The Pathway of Holiness: A Guide for Sinners*. Downers Grove, IL: InterVarsity Press, 1996.

Wilkinson, Bruce. *Personal Holiness in Times of Temptation*. Eugene, OR: Harvest House, 1998.

The Woman's Study Bible. Nashville: Thomas Nelson Publishers, 1995.

Winebrenner, Jan. *Intimate Faith: A Woman's Guide to the Spiritual Disciplines*. New York: Warner Books, 2003.

Zodhiates, Spiros. *The Hebrew–Greek Key Study Bible*. Chattanooga: AMG Publishers, 1984.

Notes

Notes

New Hope® Publishers is a division of WMU®, an international organization that challenges Christian believers to understand and be radically involved in God's mission. For more information about WMU, go to www.wmu.com. More information about New Hope books may be found at www.newhopepublishers.com. New Hope books may be purchased at your local bookstore.

If you've been blessed by this book, we would like to hear your story. The publisher and author welcome your comments and suggestions at: newhopereader@wmu.org.

Other Books in "A Woman's Guide" Series

Spiritual Wellness
A Personal Study of Colossians
Rhonda H. Kelley
"A Woman's Guide" Series – Revised Edition

True Contentment
A Biblical Study for Achieving Satisfaction in Life
Rhonda Harrington Kelley
ISBN-10: 1-59669-260-X
ISBN-13: 978-1-59669-260-2

Spiritual Wellness
A Personal Study of Colossians
Rhonda Harrington Kelley
ISBN-10: 1-59669-259-6
ISBN-13: 978-1-59669-259-6

Available in bookstores everywhere.

For information about these books or any New Hope product, visit www.newhopepublishers.com.